ENDANGERED SPECIES

CHRISTOPHER LAMPTON

ENDANGERED SPECIES

FRANKLIN WATTS   AN IMPACT BOOK
NEW YORK/LONDON/TORONTO/SYDNEY/1988

Photographs courtesy of: Photo Researchers, Inc.: pp. 28 (National Audubon Society), 32 (Toni Angermayer), 38 (H. Silvester/Rapho), 43 (George Holton), 47 (Jen and Des Bartlett), 60 (Gordon S. Smith/National Audubon Society), 63 (top—Dr. Jeremy Burgess/Science Photo Library), 63 (bottom left—DeCasseres), 63 (bottom right—R. Borneman), 78 (Carl D. Koford/National Audubon Society), 81 (George Laycock); American Museum of Natural History: p. 41; TVA: pp. 74, 75.

Library of Congress Cataloging-in-Publication Data
Lampton, Christopher.
Endangered species / Christopher Lampton.
p.   cm. — (An impact book)
Bibliography: p.
Includes index.
Summary: Explains what species are, how they become extinct, and the effect of extinction on the ecology, and surveys endangered species of plants and animals and possible solutions.
ISBN 0-531-10510-5
1. Endangered species—Juvenile literature. 2. Extinction (Biology)—Juvenile literature. 3. Wildlife conservation—Juvenile literature. [1. Rare animals. 2. Rare Plants. 3. Extinction (Biology) 4. Wildlife conservation.] I. Title.
QL83.L36 1988   87-25161 CIP AC
574—dc19

CONTENTS

ENDANGERED SPECIES

INTRODUCTION
THE GREAT DYING
REVISITED

There are some things that money can't buy.

One of them is a dinosaur. Try though you might, you'll never find a living dinosaur for sale, not even in the Neiman-Marcus catalog. In fact, you'll never find a dinosaur, for sale or not. If you're lucky, you might find enough pieces of a dinosaur to put together a skeleton, but that's all. Dinosaurs lived on this planet a long time ago, and now they are gone. Nothing can bring them back.

Of course, everybody knows that you can't buy a dinosaur. Dinosaurs are extinct. They became extinct 65 million years ago, wiped out by a vast catastrophe that we don't yet understand. And not just the dinosaurs became extinct in this "great dying"; many other species disappeared as well. Because so many species died off in a fairly short period of time, we refer to this great dying as a *mass extinction*. Scientists who study the remains of ancient life tell us that there have been several such mass extinctions in earth's long history. Nobody knows why they happen. They may be caused by sudden natural changes in the earth's climate, though one recent theory suggests that they occur like clockwork every 26 million years when the earth is bombarded by comets, giant chunks of ice from the outer fringes of the solar system—but this theory is highly controversial.

We are in the middle of a mass extinction right now. It isn't being caused by chunks of ice from space or sudden changes in the climate; it is being caused by the human race. In the late 1980s, species are dying off at a rate of more than one a day; by the early 1990s, more than one species will vanish every hour. The dawn of the twenty-first century will see *one million fewer species on this planet* than did the dawn of the twentieth. Another great dying is in progress—and very little is being done to stop it.

How did this mass extinction come about? How can we stop it? Scientists do not have to devise eleborate theories to explain this twentieth century disaster; the cause is all around them. Human beings, through exploitation and neglect and overuse of the earth's resources, are engaged in wholesale destruction of the other living organisms on this planet. We are killing off our fellow species at an alarming rate.

When a species becomes extinct, no power on earth can bring it back, just as nothing can bring back the dinosaurs. If a species of tiger ceases to exist, or a kind of flower, or an insect, not all the money on Earth can buy another one. Extinction is forever. It is worse than the death of an individual organism. When an individual dies, at least the children of that individual will survive to carry on the species. But when a species becomes extinct, there *are* no children. The dinosaurs left behind no descendants to populate this planet. Neither did the woolly mammoth, or the dodo bird, or the passenger pigeon, all of them now absent from the face of the earth. If nothing is done, they will be followed into oblivion by the giant panda, the California condor, and a million other *endangered species*—species that are teetering on the brink of extinction *at this very moment.*

Species that are nearing extinction include

• the African cheetah, displaced from its natural home as civilization encroaches on the rain forests of its native continent;
• the South American giant otter, slaughtered by hunters for its beautiful fur;
• the Asian giant panda, starving because of the loss of the bamboo it needs to survive;
• the Arctic polar bear, pursued by hunters for its fur, driven from its natural home;
• almost *every* species of whale; these huge, gentle, intelligent mammals have been hunted for their meat, their fat, their very bones, until they have nearly vanished from the oceans.

These are only a few of the most glamorous of the one million species now on the road to extinction. Many of the endangered species are plants, insects, and animals that you have never heard of, some that *no one* has ever heard of, but which nonetheless represent a valuable part of life on Earth.

This book is about the mass extinction that is now in progress. In the pages that follow, you will see how the diversity of living species on this planet came about, why this diversity is disappearing, why we should do everything in our power to stop this process, and why it is already too late to save many of the species that are about to vanish forever.

1

WHY SPECIES
EXIST

Life on Earth comes in many varieties. Look out the nearest window, and you'll see a few dozen—or a few hundred—examples.

We call these varieties *species*. Human beings are one species of living organisms, as are dogs, cats, rosebushes, crabgrass, houseflies, and mosquitoes. In general, we can tell if two living organisms are of different species because they look different.

This isn't always true. Poodles and great danes look different but are of the same species: *canis familiaris*, the domestic dog. And sometimes two organisms can look pretty much identical to the untrained eye, even though they belong to different species. The scientific rule is that two organisms are of the same species if they can interbreed, that is, if a male and a female can produce offspring. Poodles and great danes can produce offspring, so they must be of the same species. Poodles and cats, on the other hand, cannot produce offspring—even if, for some reason, they want to—and so must be of different species. But, on the whole, different species *look* different. No one, for instance, would mistake a dandelion for a gerbil, or an amoeba for a Saint Bernard.

By some estimates, there are more than 10 million different species of living organisms on this planet, most of which have never been given names. Obviously, this figure is a guess, though an educated one; it may be too large—some estimates put the figure at 4 or 5 million— or it may be too small. Most of these species are plants, and quite a few are insects; only a small portion are large animals such as mammals and birds.

Where did all these species come from? The answer lies in the distant past, in the strange chemical brew of the primeval oceans of planet Earth.

ANCIENT ORIGINS

The origin of life on Earth is a subject of some debate among scientists, but we can sketch a rough picture of how it *probably* happened.

The Earth itself was born about 4.5 billion years ago, as a cooling ball of molten rock orbiting around the still-young sun. As it cooled, the low-lying plains filled with water and became oceans. Gases erupted from volcanoes, surrounding our planet and forming the atmosphere.

These early oceans and this early atmosphere were full of chemicals that would have killed human beings instantly. But these poisonous chemicals, combined with the energy from lightning bolts and volcanoes, provided a perfect environment for the construction of brand new molecules.

A molecule is a chain of atoms, the tiny building blocks of all solids, liquids, and gases in the universe. Some of the molecules—the chains of atoms—in the primeval sea were very large, consisting of dozens, hundreds, or even thousands of atoms. When lightning bolts and unfiltered rays of sunlight struck the water, or when the water was heated by lava from a volcano, these molecules would fall apart, only to come back together in the form of new molecules.

These molecules were formed at random, but within the laws of chemistry. After hundreds of millions of years, luck and chemistry created a chain of atoms that possessed a peculiar property: it could make copies of itself.

How can a molecule make copies of itself? Looking back across 4 billion years, it's difficult to say, but we can guess that these primitive, self-replicating molecules used a technique similar to that used by a modern self-replicating molecule, the chromosome.

Your body contains trillions of these chromosomes, as do the bodies of all living things, from aardvarks to cacti to Japanese beetles. Actually, each individual human being has only forty-six *different* chromosomes, but there are trillions of copies of these chromosomes inside the human body, with each set of copies locked inside the tiny units of flesh called *cells*. When these cells split in two to make new cells, the chromosomes copy themselves so that the new cells can have chromosomes as well. To copy itself, a chromosome uses its own atoms as a mold, or template, for the construction of a new chromosome. The new chromosome is assembled from loose molecules floating around in the liquid interior of the cell.

The self-replicating molecules in the primeval sea had plenty of loose molecules—spare parts, if you will—from which to make copies of themselves. Because the copies of the original self-replicating molecule also made copies of themselves, the primeval oceans would have filled up quickly with these molecules. Before long, the molecules would have begun competing for the spare parts required to make new copies of themselves. Some molecules were better at gathering spare parts than other molecules. Copies of these faster-reproducing molecules soon came to outnumber their slower cousins—until other molecules came along that were even better at obtaining spare parts. Some of these molecules might have preyed on other self-replicating molecules, dismantling them for construction materials, the same way that modern predators prey on other organisms for food.

But wait a minute! If all of these molecules were identical copies of the original self-replicating molecule, how could some have been better at making copies of themselves than others?

The answer is that they were *not* identical. Occasionally, a molecule would make a mistake in replicating itself and produce a flawed copy. Most of these flawed copies were worthless; they were incapable even of reproducing themselves. But occasionally one of these flawed copies was actually an improvement on the original, and would become a winner in the competition for spare parts.

Thus, over millions and billions of years, the self-replicating molecules steadily improved themselves, through a combination of random mistakes (which we call *mutations*) and the harsh requirements of surviving in the world around them (which we call *environmental pressures*). In time, the molecules discovered the advantage of teaming together with other molecules to form cells. And eventually some cells teamed together with other cells to form multi-celled organisms. Human beings are multi-celled organisms, as are all other living things large enough to be seen with the naked eye.

This combination of mutation and environmental pressure is called *natural selection*. It is the driving force behind the slow process of change called *evolution*, by which organisms are gradually adapted for the environment—the surroundings—in which they live.

WORKING TOGETHER

As the self-replicating organisms developed more and more sophisticated ways of surviving in their environments, they also branched out to form more and more different kinds—that is, species—of organisms. This process is called *speciation*. It has occurred many, many times since living molecules first formed in the primeval ocean, as evidenced by the many different species found on Earth today. And yet the species on our planet today represent only a fraction of the species that have existed over the last 4 billion years.

Just as the self-replicating molecules competed with one another for the spare parts they needed for making copies of themselves, modern living organisms sometimes compete with one another for the necessities of their own survival—food, shelter, energy. But competition is unstable. One species quickly loses the competition and either dies out or is chased into a different environment.

Cooperation is just as common and it *is* stable. Organisms that cooperate in the ways that they use the environment, or at least don't produce conflict, can live together for long periods of time. If you study a natural environment, you will see many examples of cooperation. One example of cooperation is the food chain.

In order to survive, living organisms need energy. Energy is the force that allows the organisms, and the molecules of which they are constructed, to move. Even plants, which sometimes seem to be completely stationary, are full of movement on the molecular level. The first self-replicating molecules received their energy from the bolts of lightning and the volcanoes and storms that jostled the oceans, but organisms today need another source. That source is the sun.

Unfortunately, we cannot simply walk outside on a sunny day and absorb solar energy while we get a tan. Only one type of organism can use the sun's energy directly: green plants.

When the light from the sun strikes the surface of a green plant, the plant "traps" the sun's energy through a process called *photosynthesis* (from Greek words meaning, literally, "to create with light"). This energy is then stored in molecules called *carbohydrates*, so that the plant can use it later to power the activity of its cells.

An animal that eats the plant transfers the carbohydrates to its own body and can use the energy in the carbohydrates to power its own cells. (This isn't the only reason that animals eat plants—the molecules in the plant are also used by the animal as "spare parts" for building cells—but it is the single most important reason.) An animal that eats the animal that ate the plant will also receive the energy from the carbohydrates. Thus the sun's energy is passed from plant to herbivorous ("plant-eating") animal to carnivorous ("meat-eating") animal. This is the food chain.

If it weren't for plants, animals could not live. The plants perform the important service of capturing the sun's energy and putting it into a form that can be used by those of us who aren't capable of photosynthesis. You might question, though, whether this is really a form of cooperation. Are the plants building carbohydrates as a favor for animals—or are the animals stealing the carbohydrates from the plants? Do the plants *want* to be eaten?

In many cases, the answer is no. In fact, some plants have evolved elaborate defenses—thorns, poisons, foul-tasting leaves—to prevent animals from eating them. (Of course, animals have in turn evolved ways of eating these plants anyway!) But in other cases, the plants produce fruits and vegetables that are *intended* as food for animals. The fruits and vegetables contain seeds, and, when the animals eat them, they spread the seeds, in their waste matter or through sloppy eating, into places these seeds could not otherwise reach. The animals receive carbohydrate energy and molecular spare parts; the plants have their offspring spread to remote corners of the landscape. By cooperating, both parties come out ahead in the evolutionary sweepstakes.

So complex are the interrelationships among living

species that a given environment—a meadow or a swamp or even a desert—is like a finely tooled machine in which every organism plays a part. If even a single organism is removed from the environment, the machine will suffer. If enough organisms are removed, the machine will fall apart, and the environment will die. In a sense, an environment is like a large super-organism, and the individual organisms within the environment are the "cells" and "molecules" that make it up.

The study of environments and the individual organisms that make them up is called *ecology*. The environments themselves, along with the organisms that live in them, are called *ecosystems*.

How do ecosystems come into existence? They are the result of many millions of years of experimenting on the part of nature to find a mixture of living things that can live together in a stable environment. Most of these experiments are unsuccessful; what we see when we look at nature are the combinations that worked, the end products of considerable trial and error.

Ecosystems are also the result of millions of years of adaptation on the part of individual organisms. Natural selection tends to favor organisms that find cooperative rather than competitive ways of fitting into their environments. Thus, each organism must find its ecological niche— a way in which it can survive in an ecosystem without conflicting with the ways in which other organisms survive in that ecosystem. For instance, two different grazing animals that live together on the African plain may both eat grass, but if they evolve to eat different *kinds* of grass they can live peaceably together, because they do not compete. The kind of grass or other food that an organism eats, the kind of shelter it requires, and the way in which it rears its young, all constitute its ecological niche.

As organisms have evolved to be better adapted to

the environments in which they live, they have developed powerful tools to enhance their own adaptability. One of the most formidable of these tools is sexual reproduction.

SPREADING
THE GENES

Although all living organisms today descended from those first self-replicating molecules in the primeval sea, the parts of our bodies that most resemble those original molecules are the chromosomes in our cells. And these chromosomes are probably the most important part of any living organism today.

The chromosomes contain information, written in a language called the *genetic code*. In effect, the chromosomes are like a recipe book. They contain the instructions for building all of the molecules that make up the living creature of which the chromosome is a part. Each of these molecular "recipes" is called a *gene*. Special molecular "machines" inside the cells read these recipes and convert them into molecules.

If two organisms belong to the same species, then the genes in their chromosomes will be very similar, because they both require the same molecules in their bodies. But the genes will not be identical, because individuals are never identical. Some human beings, for instance, have blue eyes and others have brown eyes; this reflects a difference in the genes that contain the recipes for the pigment molecules in the eye. In the same way, individuals with brown hair have different hair color genes than individuals with blond hair or red hair or black hair.

When an organism produces offspring—that is, has children—it passes on copies of its genes so that the offspring's body will also be capable of building the molecules it needs to survive. However, if the organism practices sexual reproduction—and most organisms do—then each offspring will receive genes from *two* parents, in a random combination. The child of a blue-eyed father and a brown-eyed mother may receive blue eyes or brown eyes, depending on which parent it receives its eye-color gene from. (As we shall see in a moment, it is also possible for the child to receive an eye color different from either parent's eye color.)

Why is it important for genes to be shuffled around in this manner? If all members of a species had exactly the same genes, then they would be able to live in only a single kind of environment, the kind of environment that those genes are adapted for. But if the species carries many different kinds of genes, and different members of the species receive different combinations of those genes, then that species will be able to live in several different environments. If one environment is destroyed, some members of the species will be able to adapt to other environments. The total set of genes carried by all members of a species is called the *gene pool*. The more diversity in the gene pool—that is, the more varieties of genes that are available—the more likely that the species will be able to adapt to changing environments.

It's important to note the way in which genes are passed on from one generation to the next. Although we implied earlier that every organism has one gene for each characteristic, this isn't actually true. Each organism has *two* genes for each characteristic, one from each parent. How does the organism know which gene recipe to use? Well, if both of the genes are identical—that is, if they contain recipes for identical molecules—then there is no conflict. It doesn't matter which one is used. But if they are different, then the machinery inside the cell that builds molecules must decide which recipe to use. Fortunately, some genes are better at getting themselves used (or *expressed*) than others. The genes that are good at getting themselves expressed are called *dominant* genes. Genes that are not as good at getting themselves expressed are called *recessive* genes. When the cellular machinery must choose between two different genes, it always chooses the dominant gene. For instance, a human being with genes for both blue eyes and brown eyes will have brown eyes, because brown eyes are dominant over blue eyes. Recessive genes express themselves only when an individual receives them from *both* parents. (This is why an individual can express characteristics, such as eye color, that were expressed by neither parent, if both parents carried recessive genes for that characteristic.)

New genes enter a gene pool through mutation—that is, through an accident that occurs when a chromosome makes a copy of itself. Some of these new genes are improvements on the original, and will quickly spread through the population, because they will increase the organism's chances of surviving in its environment and of producing offspring. But most of the new genes will be bad. If these bad genes are dominant genes, they will disappear rapidly from the gene pool, because the individuals who inherit them will die before they are able to produce offspring. But if they are recessive, they may spread through the population, because many of the individuals who receive them will not express them. Only when two organisms who both carry the bad genes produce offspring will the offspring express the bad characteristic. This, for instance, is how genetic diseases such as hemophilia and cystic fibrosis spread through the human population. (For this reason, there are laws preventing closely related individuals, such as siblings and first cousins, from marrying. The chances are too great that they might be carrying the same recessive genes.)

Fortunately, if a population of a species is very large, the odds of two individuals who both carry bad genes coming together and producing offspring are small. Thus, large and medium-sized populations are generally healthier than small populations. In fact, if the population of a species grows *very* small, it will begin to suffer from *inbreeding depression*—too many recessive genes expressing themselves in too many individuals. Unless the size of such a population can be quickly increased, inbreeding depression can mean rapid extinction.

But extinction is the subject of the next chapter. Now that we've seen why species exist and how they live together, let's look at the other side of the coin—how species *cease* to exist.

HOW SPECIES BECOME EXTINCT

Slightly less than 2 million years ago, the Earth entered a period of its long history that scientists term the *Pleistocene epoch*. The Pleistocene lasted until about 10,000 years ago, practically into modern times. (The current period of planetary history is known as the *Holocene*, or *recent*, *epoch*.) The Pleistocene was distinguished by two events—the rise of a new species called *homo sapiens*, and the rise and extinction of an unusual number of large land animals.

These events—the extinction of the large land animals and the rise of the human race—were not coincidental. They were a cause and an effect. Human beings (along with certain changes in climate) were directly responsible for the extinction of the Pleistocene megafauna—the large land animals of the Pleistocene epoch—at least according to many scientists who study the prehistoric past.

The newly evolved *homo sapiens* was the greatest hunter the world had yet known, greater than the Tyrannosaurus Rex, greater than the saber-toothed tiger. Though the early humans may have lacked the fangs, claws, and ferocity of their animal counterparts, they made up for this lack in sheer ingenuity. They built weapons to compensate for what they lacked physically, and teamed up to accomplish what a lone hunter could not. The woolly mammoth, the mastodon, the saber-toothed tiger and other creatures hunted to extinction by *homo sapiens* never had a chance.

At the end of the Pleistocene, most humans hung up their hunting gear and settled down to a more sedate existence as farmers, domesticating the animals whose flesh they ate. Yet humans are still responsible for the extinctions of other species. How? By applying deadly pressures, either deliberate or inadvertent, on those species, threatening their continued survival.

Until the coming of human beings, animal extinctions—such as the mass extinctions that brought about the demise of the dinosaurs and other species in the prehistoric past—were the result of natural events, whether those events were cosmic disasters or changes in the environment in which those species lived. Now *we* have become the chief cause of extinctions. Although natural disasters still occasionally wreak havoc in the animal and plant kingdoms, most extinctions in the last few centuries have been the result of human intervention in the natural world.

There are many different ways in which human beings can apply deadly pressure on other species. In the next few pages, we'll look at a variety of these ways.

OVERHUNTING

The day of the Pleistocene hunter is long gone, but humans still hunt—for food, for sport, and for animal by-products such as furs and oils. At least one animal, the rhinoceros, is hunted because superstitious people believe that parts of its body will cure diseases—they will not—or improve their love lives, which is even less likely. Because of the proficiency and skill of human hunters, any hunted animal is in danger of extinction, unless extraordinary steps are taken to control the hunters. And hunters are notoriously difficult to control!

The most spectacular example of an animal hunted to extinction—since the Pleistocene, anyway—occurred within the memory of people alive today. The victim was the passenger pigeon, once the most common bird in North America, and possibly the most common bird on Earth.

The passenger pigeon was a large pigeon that lived in the forests of North America. When the first settlers arrived on the continent, they found what Samuel de Champlain, the French explorer, called "an infinite number of pigeons," an estimate that wasn't as farfetched as it sounds. The total population of passenger pigeons was certainly in the billions, and they migrated northward and southward across the continent in flocks of more than 100 million birds. When they flew across the sky, the sun would vanish, and night would seem to fall. They could do considerable damage to a forest just by settling onto the branches of its trees, and when they moved on, the ground would be buried under several feet of droppings. When they flew together, the flapping of their wings was "like the roar of distant thunder," according to the famous naturalist John James Audubon.

Obviously, the passenger pigeon was a successful species, well adapted to its environment. But, in a world dominated by human beings, it had made a crucial evolutionary mistake: it was delicious to eat. Purveyors of gourmet food were willing to pay cash on the barrelhead for dead passenger pigeons, and greedy hunters were more than willing to supply the carcasses.

The birds had not evolved to resist that modern weapon of destruction, the gun. As the passenger pigeons migrated, parties of hunters would wait for them in their nesting grounds and slaughter them wholesale as they alighted amid the trees. The dead and dying pigeons

could then be bagged and carried off. A party of hunters could easily kill fifty thousand birds in a week.

But even wholesale slaughter seemed insufficient to exterminate a species as common as the passenger pigeon. How could mere human beings armed with guns threaten the future of a species that numbered in the billions?

Quite easily, as it turned out. No one knows when the slaughter of the passenger pigeon began, though it was probably shortly after settlers began to arrive in the sixteenth and seventeenth centuries. But the end of the slaughter is quite easy to pinpoint. On March 24, 1900, a young hunter shot the last passenger pigeon ever seen in the wild. For some years afterward, a few of the birds survived in zoos, but on September 1, 1914, the last passenger pigeon in captivity died in the Cincinnati Zoo. The species was extinct.

The story of the passenger pigeon is extraordinary, but it isn't all *that* extraordinary. Many other species have met the same fate: overhunted into extinction. In fact, it is a sad refrain that recurs throughout human history. Other animals hunted into oblivion in recent centuries include the quagga (a close relative of the zebra), the aurochs (a relative of the bison), and Steller's sea cow (a relative of the manatee, probably responsible for some reported sightings of "mermaids"). In the last century, the American bison, sometimes incorrectly called the

The passenger pigeon, once the most common bird in North America, was hunted to extinction in the nineteenth century. The last passenger pigeon died in captivity in 1914. This engraving is from a watercolor executed by the nineteenth-century wildlife artist John J. Audubon.

American buffalo, was nearly hunted into extinction. Fortunately, most varieties of this animal have managed to recover from overhunting and are, at least temporarily, out of risk.

Alas, the overhunting of animals continues, and many animals are even now in danger of being hunted out of existence. And nowhere since the extermination of the passenger pigeon has overhunting been carried to such extremes as in the whaling industry.

Whales, the largest animals on earth and one of the most intelligent, have been hunted in great numbers for centuries. Historically, the carcasses of the whales have been used for many things. The fat is melted down for oil, the meat is processed as food, even the bones have found uses. And because of their size, even a single whale represents a large income for a shipload of whale hunters.

So it is not surprising that whale hunting has proceeded at a fierce rate since at least the seventeenth century. The earliest European whalers pursued the Atlantic right whale, so called because it was easy to kill, rich with oil and bone, and therefore the "right" whale for the whalers to hunt. More than a century ago, the Atlantic right was hunted to commercial extinction—that is, the point at which there were too few whales left for profitable hunting. Over the centuries, the whalers have similarly pursued the Pacific right whale, the Atlantic sperm whale, and the bowhead whale, pushing each to the verge of extinction. As the large (and therefore highly profitable) whales have vanished from the oceans, smaller and smaller whales have been hunted.

As the number of whales has decreased, the technology used in their pursuit has become more and more sophisticated: faster ships, longer-range harpoons with explosive tips. In the first half of this century, tens of thousands of whales were killed every year.

In recent decades, international treaties have protected many species of whale from exploitation and placed quotas on the hunting of others; but not all nations have honored these treaties, and outlaw whalers have continued to hunt whales as though the treaties did not exist.

Just as the passenger pigeon was brought to extinction because it made a tasty meal, many animals are threatened by the beauty of their pelts, which are used to make fur coats and other luxury items. In South America, the jaguar, a favorite source of fur, is in danger of extinction after intense hunting in the 1960s. The Asian tiger and the snow leopard are similarly threatened.

The Guadalupe fur seal was believed to be extinct on two separate occasions. However, it still survives in small numbers on an island off California, where its existence is threatened by poachers. The Pribilof fur seal off the Alaskan coast has been hunted for 150 years, despite the fact that the Pribilof Islands, where the seals live, were declared off limits to seal hunters more than a century ago.

Other species endangered by fur hunting include the Andean vicuna, the Australian red kangaroo, the cheetah of Africa, as well as the African black and white Colobus monkeys, the Barbary leopard, the South American giant otter and several of its smaller relatives, the chinchilla—and far too many other furbearing animals to list here.

The list of profitable reasons for hunting animals is nearly endless. Turtles are hunted for their shells, other reptiles for their exotic skins (which can be turned into clothing, handbags, shoes, and an endless assortment of trinkets). Rare birds are hunted so that they can be sold as pets; wild deer, manatees, and game birds for their tasty meat. The rhinoceros is hunted for just about every part of its body.

On close examination, it might seem that hunters who exterminate a species are working against their own best

interests. An industry, such as the whaling industry, that makes its income from a commercially valuable animal species would seem to have a vested interest in *preventing* that animal from becoming extinct. If the animals disappear, so does the hunter's income.

And, in fact, there are international organizations founded by hunters and dedicated to finding ways of perpetuating the existence of hunted species. The International Whaling Commission attempts to prevent overhunting of whales. The International Fur Trade Confederation performs a similar role in the protection of furbearing species. These organizations do not attempt to ban all hunting of these species—such a ban would, after all, put an end to the very industries that these organizations are designed to protect—but they do have authority to regulate which animals can be hunted, which are endangered, and which are subject to hunting quotas.

But not all hunters see such regulations as being in their self-interest. The sad fact is that sometimes extermination of a species *is* profitable, even if it is morally reprehensible. If the whalers exterminated every whale on Earth today and invested the earnings from their carcasses at compound interest, they would almost certainly earn more *in the long run* from the compound interest than from placing rational limits on whaling that would ensure the survival of the whales. And there will always be renegade hunters—poachers—who wish to turn a quick profit for themselves at the expense of other hunters— and of the species that they destroy.

The magnificent Sibirischer tiger. The tiger, prized for its fur, has been hunted to the point of extinction.

It's only fair to add that some small-scale hunting is performed by people who need food or fur in order to survive. Eskimos, for instance, have traditionally hunted whales for food and blubber and killed seals for clothing. This kind of hunting is much easier to condone than hunting performed purely for profit rather than need. But this small-scale hunting is also less likely to endanger the future of a species.

Not all hunting of endangered species is practiced for profit. Some of it is simply for fun—or sport, as the hunters themselves might prefer to phrase it. Sport hunting at its most excessive can be every bit as destructive as hunting for profit. In centuries past, wealthy hunters have boasted of killing animals in numbers that seem astonishing (and not a little disgusting) by modern standards. One nineteenth century English hunter supposedly killed five hundred thousand animals in his lifetime! In some instances, this hunting scarcely represented sport: a wealthy Maharajah would have the animals led to his side one at a time by bearers, so that he could place a gun against each animal's head and kill it with a single shot, in order to prove how virile and brave he was.

In the Middle East, an animal called the oryx (believed to be the origin of the unicorn legend, because of its long horns) has been hunted for centuries by Arabs. Legend has it that a person who kills an oryx will receive the animal's courage and strength. In modern times, however, the oryx hunt has consisted of several hunters in a jeep firing machine guns at a fleeing oryx—hardly proof of anyone's courage and skill. Because of this hunting, the oryx no longer exists in the wild except in special reserves, where it is protected from machine gun–wielding "hunters."

During a five-year period in the mid-1970s, nearly all of the thirty thousand elephants in Uganda were exterminated by gun-wielding troops in one of the greatest animal massacres of modern times—despite the fact that the elephant was protected by law as an endangered species.

The American bison was the victim of a similar, if more extensive, massacre in the nineteenth century. The motivation, however, was not entirely sport; the United States government apparently encouraged the near extermination of the bison because it represented an important food source of the American Indians, with whom the government was perpetually at war.

Some animals are hunted neither for sport nor for profit, but because they are perceived, rightly or wrongly, as a threat or a nuisance.

Wolves have been a frequent victim of this kind of persecution, because farmers and ranchers believe they prey on their livestock, a reputation the wolves have not always deserved. Grizzly bears have been hunted for similar reasons, as have cougars and coyotes. Many subspecies of these animals have been driven to extinction. (A *subspecies* is a variety of an animal that can still interbreed with other varieties, though it is not physically identical to those varieties.)

Worse, the persecution of these animals is often a threat to other animals. Poisoning of predators, for instance, is a threat not only to the predators, but also to animals who eat the poisoned carcasses of the predators. And the decimation of one species can have a negative effect on other animals who depend on that species for food, as is the case with the prairie dog and the blackfooted ferret, as we shall see later in this chapter.

DESTRUCTION OF HABITAT

Hunting represents the *deliberate* decimation (if not necessarily the deliberate extermination) of a species. (The word *decimation* means, literally, to remove every tenth member of a species. We use the word here to mean the reduction but not necessarily the endangering of a species.) Although many species are threatened, or have already been driven to extinction, by overhunting and persecution, far more species on this planet are *inadvertently* threatened. And the most common inadvertent threats come from destruction of habitat.

We saw in the last chapter that species evolve over long periods of time to fit into their ecosystems. The particular *kind* of ecosystem to which a species has adapted is referred to as that species' *habitat*. Some species—human beings are an especially good example—have evolved to fit a wide variety of habitats. But many species need a particular *kind* of habitat in order to survive or to perform certain important biological activities. Many animals and plants can survive only in wetlands, or in fresh water, or in forests. When such a species loses its habitat, the species itself must die.

Certain habitats on this planet, such as wetlands and forests, are being slowly destroyed in order to make room for human development. As these habitats are destroyed, the species that need these habitats for their survival are being brought closer and closer to extinction.

Nowhere is this problem more acute than in the tropical areas around the Earth's equator. Why? Because most of the species found on Earth today are found in tropical rain forests—and because these rain forests are the sites of wholesale habitat destruction.

The tropical rain forests are an amazing environment. They are found on both sides of the world—in Asia and Africa in the east, in South and Central America in the west. They cover roughly 3.5 million square miles (9.1 sq km) of Earth's surface. They contain a vast array of life forms, both animal and vegetable. Trees in a rain forest can tower more than 100 feet (30 m) in height. Below these giant trees grow several levels of smaller trees. Within a rain forest can be found dozens or even hundreds of different *micro-climates*, mini-ecosystems each of which contains its own unique collection of plant and animal species.

And the rain forests are vanishing. By some estimates, nearly half of the rain forests that existed a century ago have already been cut down, and more are being destroyed, at a rate of 43,000 square miles (111,000 sq km) per year, an area roughly half the size of Pennsylvania. Within half a century, there may be no rain forests left at all. And for every square mile of rain forest that is removed, untold thousands of plants are killed, and an important animal habitat is lost. Since no one has yet cataloged all of the plant species that exist in the rain forests, it is difficult to say how often a species of rain forest plant becomes extinct, but it must be a common event.

Why are the rain forests being removed? Mostly, to make way for farms. And what is being raised on these farms? In South America, the answer is primarily cattle, to supply beef for fast food restaurants in North America. The most prolific natural environment on Earth is being traded for cheap hamburgers.

Ironically, the rain forests are a poor environment for farming. In North America, the soil left behind when a forest is cleared is rich with nutrients and provides fertile land for farming. But most of the nutrients in a rain forest are contained within the plants themselves, not the soil. When the trees and other plants are chopped down, they leave behind an especially poor soil for farming.

This problem can be alleviated somewhat by *burning* the trees and allowing the ash to enrich the soil. (This technique is known, for good reason, as *slash and burn agriculture*.) Even so, the farmlands created by the destruction of rain forest are good, at best, for two or three years of farming and grazing; then more rain forest must be destroyed to create more farmland. Thus the destruction of the rain forests is an ongoing process that will end

*Slash and burn agriculture, such as the example
shown in this photo from the Amazon region
of Brazil, results in the destruction of rain forests,
home to millions of plant and animal species.*

only when the rain forests are no more. And when the rain forests die, millions of species that exist only in rain forests will die with them.

Among large land animals, the group most threatened by the destruction of the rain forests are the cats. Of approximately twenty-five different species of cats that live in tropical rain forests, fifteen are in danger of extinction as those rain forests are taken away from them. But the majority of the species that live in the rain forests are not animals but plants, in literally millions of varieties, most of which have never been cataloged by botanists. These plants exist *only* in the rain forest, many of them only in small portions of the rain forest, and will cease to exist when the rain forests cease to exist.

Another type of environment being rapidly destroyed is the *wetland*, swamps and marshes found both in the tropics and in the temperate zones to their north and south. Wetlands serve as the breeding grounds for many fish, birds, and other animals.

Because the soil beneath the waters is rich, wetlands are commonly filled in to create farms, a fate much like that of the tropical rain forests. At the turn of the century, the United States boasted more than 120 million acres (48 million ha) of wetlands; by the mid-1980s, that number had been reduced to 80 million acres (32 million ha).

As the wetlands vanish, the species that need the wetlands vanish, lost to the same fate as the denizens of the rain forests.

CHANGES IN THE ENVIRONMENT

It's not necessary to completely destroy a habitat in order to disrupt the lives of the species that live there. Sometimes relatively small changes to an environment are enough to wreak havoc with species that have spent millions of years evolving to fit that environment. This is illustrated most vividly where species have developed in a completely closed environment, such as an island.

Islands play an important role in speciation (which, you'll recall, is the creation of new species). When members of a species become completely, or almost completely, isolated from others of their kind, they are free to evolve in new directions. If this separation continues for a long enough period of time, the organisms may evolve into a brand new species, incapable of breeding with their relatives elsewhere, even should they be reunited.

Charles Darwin, the brilliant naturalist who introduced the concept of natural selection in the nineteenth century, noticed this phenomenon while visiting the Galápagos Islands in his youth. Each island, he observed, had its own unique species of finch, a small species of bird, different from the finches on all other islands in the chain. Darwin theorized that these finches had originally migrated from the mainland thousands of years earlier, perhaps blown out to sea by savage storms. Each had subsequently evolved along separate lines until new species of finch, or at least new subspecies, had developed.

Since new species evolve more readily on islands than elsewhere, you might guess that a large percentage of the species on this planet are found on islands. And you would be right.

The finches of the Galápagos Islands, arranged to show the evolutionary tree of their development. When Charles Darwin visited the islands in the nineteenth century, he discovered that each island had its own unique species of finch.

But island ecology is fragile indeed. It doesn't take much to disrupt an island ecosystem. Because plants and animals on an island have relatively few predators—in some cases, in fact, they have no natural predators at all—they evolve few defenses against predators. So the introduction of even a single predator species to an island environment can be disastrous.

Sailors of centuries past had a habit of leaving pigs and goats on isolated islands, to supply nourishment for other sailors who might be shipwrecked there at a later date—or so that they themselves would have food should they ever have occasion to return. Inadvertently, they left behind a trail of ecological havoc, as the pigs and goats plowed unhindered into ecosystems that had no defenses against them.

One such disruption of an island environment, in the seventeenth century, brought about the most famous extinction of modern times, that of the dodo bird. The dodo, a large, flightless relative of the dove, was unique to the island of Mauritius, 500 miles (800 km) west of Madagascar in the Indian Ocean. Explorers from Europe discovered the dodo at the end of the sixteenth century. By the end of the seventeenth century, they had driven it to extinction.

Certainly the dodo was one of the oddest birds of modern times. Although faintly turkeylike, it was larger than a turkey and had a huge head with an oddly shaped bill. It had apparently descended from doves that had colonized the island thousands of years earlier, probably blown there by storms (like Darwin's finches in the Ga-

The dodo, a large, flightless bird that once lived on the island of Mauritius in the Indian Ocean, is now extinct.

lápagos). On Mauritius, it had no natural enemies and, therefore, had evolved no natural defenses (or had lost the ones it originally had). It couldn't fly, it moved slowly, and it wasn't very intelligent—so it easily fell prey to the dogs brought to the island by explorers. And, though descriptions of the dodo's tastiness vary somewhat from one account to another, the sailors who came to Mauritius did not hesitate to add the easily captured dodos to their diets; to them, the dodo must have seemed a delicious treat, after months of eating only shipboard supplies. Capturing a dodo was a simple matter of walking up behind the bird and bashing it on the head with a wooden club.

It's little wonder that the dodo became extinct; by 1680 the last dodo was gone. Within another hundred years, the bird was nearly forgotten as well, regarded as a myth invented by imaginative sailors, in a class with mermaids and sea serpents. However, a rediscovered cache of dodo bones proved that it really had existed.

The dodo was well-adapted for its environment, but it lived in an unusually peaceful ecosystem. When that peaceful ecosystem was disrupted by other animals—dogs, pigs, and, most especially, human beings—the dodo was unable to cope. Although the dodo is an unusual example of failure to adapt to a changing environment, it can be seen as symbolic of all endangered species, unable to cope in a world increasingly dominated—and altered—by human beings.

The most spectacular of all island environments can be found on the most spectacular of all islands: Madagascar. Even the story of Madagascar's birth is spectacular.

The continents and islands of Earth are not fixed and unmoving, as the map of the world makes them appear. Rather, they are in constant motion, sliding about like giant rafts on Earth's semi-liquid *mantle*. For a brief period around 180 million years ago, all of the continents on

Earth came together to form one mighty supercontinent; then that supercontinent broke apart to form the separate continents that we know today.

In that long-ago era, Madagascar was part of the land mass that we now call Africa, but sometime in the last 100 million years, it split off from the rest of Africa and drifted eastward. It is now 250 miles (400 km) east of Africa and still drifting, though much too slowly to be noticeable. In its 1,000-mile (1,600-km) length can be found a host of evolutionary wonders.

When Madagascar was last in contact with the continents of the world, mammals—now the dominant type of large animal on Earth—had just begun to evolve, and the primate ancestors of human beings had not yet appeared. Evolution on Madagascar took its own course; unsurprisingly, human beings did not evolve there, but the lemur, the most ancient of primates surviving into modern times, thrived. (Its ancestors probably swam or floated to Madagascar when it still lay close to the African mainland.) Giant birds also evolved in the vast Madagascan forests, including what was probably the largest bird ever to walk on this planet's surface (much too big to *fly* over that surface): the *Aepyornis*, or elephant bird, possibly the model for the Roc of the Sinbad stories. The *Aepyornis* weighed up to 1,000 pounds (495 kg) and stood up to 10 feet (3 m) tall. (It was not as tall as the now extinct *dinornis*, or giant moa, of New Zealand, which reached heights of 13 feet (4 m), but it was considerably heavier.) Its eggs were big enough to contain two hundred average-sized chicken eggs.

Because evolution on Madagascar proceeded for so long on a path separate from that followed by evolution elsewhere, the island produced a host of species found nowhere else in the world: 99 percent of the Madagascan reptiles are unique, as are 81 percent of its flowering plants, and 99 percent of its frogs. And, because the Madagascan landscape features a number of different environments—desert, rain forest, and dry forest—the variety of these species is also great.

Many centuries ago, human beings arrived on Madagascar and inexorably began to disrupt the ecosystem. In this century, advances in medical technology have allowed the human population of Madagascar, the Malagasy peoples, to grow by leaps and bounds. As a result, human beings have come more and more to encroach on the impressive evolutionary experiments that nature has performed on Madagascar.

When humans arrived, 90 percent of Madagascar was covered with forest; now the forests cover only 10 percent. Most of this forest has been torn down to make room for farmland, so that the people of Madagascar can be fed. While it's hard to argue with the need for farms, this wholesale loss of habitat has resulted in a high level of extinctions on Madagascar. At least ten species of lemur have become extinct in recent centuries; twenty-one remain, but more than half of these are in danger of extinction. The elephant bird, described above, became extinct long ago, probably around 1700.

The loss of the forests is exacerbated by a high degree of erosion, a wearing away of the land itself caused by wind and rain, which is destroying the existing farmland at a rate of 2 million acres (80,000 ha) a year. According to a report published by the World Bank, Madagascar's erosion problem is the worst on Earth. To replace the farmland destroyed by erosion, still more forests must be

*The ring-tailed lemur of
Madagascar. Lemurs are
the most ancient of primates
surviving in modern times.*

destroyed. Emergency efforts are being made to save the unique species of Madagascar from what seems to be their inevitable fate, but under the circumstances only so much can be done. One ecological expert calls the Madagascar problem "the single highest conservation priority in the world."

It is not necessary that a species live on an island in order to have its life fatally disrupted by a single change in the environment. Consider the case of the black-footed ferret.

The black-footed ferret is one of the rarest mammals in North America. It attained that distinction because of its extremely narrow, inflexible ecological niche, revolving around the prairie dog. The black-footed ferret eats only prairie dogs. It even lives in abandoned prairie dog dens.

In the 1930s, an extensive campaign was waged to exterminate the prairie dog, which was regarded by farmers as a destructive pest. The black-footed ferret, already rare, became rarer still as its source of food vanished. (Eating poisoned prairie dog carcasses didn't help the ferret population either.) By the 1960s, the black-footed ferret was believed to be extinct, but this belief turned out to be premature. In September of 1981, a colony of the ferrets was discovered in Meeteetse, Wyoming, where prairie dog communities still thrived. The colony was small, numbering barely more than 100 individuals. Alas, in 1984 the colony was struck by disease, and its numbers were cut in half. At this writing, the future of the black-footed ferret hangs by the slenderest of threads. There may be no way to save it from extinction.

The giant panda of Asia has recently fallen victim to a fate similar to that of the black-footed ferret, though the change in its environment was natural, not caused by humans. The primary staple of the panda's diet is bamboo; when the bamboo crop was unexpectedly decimated, the pandas were faced with starvation. Although the panda has survived thus far, its fate is still uncertain.

POLLUTION

Pollution occurs when something finds its way into an ecosystem that doesn't belong in that ecosystem. By that definition, of course, human beings could be considered a form of pollution when they find their way into environments, such as islands, where they do not belong. But we'll use the term a little more narrowly to refer to chemicals and artificially manufactured materials that find their way into ecosystems with destructive results. The pollution of ecosystems is an increasingly deadly threat to animals and plants, endangered or otherwise.

Ecosystems are remarkably hardy. When an ecosystem is polluted by alien, organic—that is, formerly living—materials, it can generally cope with any problems that the pollution might cause. Usually, the organic materials will be degraded by microscopic organisms, which break the polluting materials into their basic components and return them to the soil, where they are recycled into the living organisms of the ecosystem.

Few ecosystems, however, are equipped to handle nonliving, chemical pollutants. When these materials enter the ecosystem, they cannot be broken down and recycled. If they are deadly, then the threat that they present will remain in the ecosystem for a long, long time.

Some of the worst chemical pollutants are the insecticides. Originally developed in the 1940s to deal with insect pests, the insecticides have proved to have side effects within the ecosystems in which they are introduced that are far worse than anything caused by the insects they were designed to exterminate.

The first popular insecticide put into general use had the tongue-twisting name dichloro-diphenyl-trichloro-ethane, but it was better known as DDT. It was hailed as a method of controlling malaria, a very deadly disease spread in tropical regions by mosquitoes, and as a way in which farmers could increase their crop yields by killing off insects that destroyed vegetables before they could be harvested. But it soon turned out that DDT was killing off more than just insects.

DDT quickly works its way deep into an ecosystem, infesting first the plants and then the animals that eat the plants and then the animals that eat the animals that eat the plants—in short, by hitching a ride on the food chain. The most common victims of DDT are fish and birds, but even those species that are not directly killed by DDT often became endangered anyway. When birds ingest DDT and its relatives, the chemicals find their way into the shells of the birds' eggs, which become so fragile that they crack open before the chicks can hatch. Unable to reproduce, several bird species—including the American bald eagle and the peregrine falcon—have become endangered by DDT.

Controls placed on the use of DDT and other insecticides have helped to reduce the peril. Both the bald eagle and the peregrine falcon have pulled back from the brink of extinction and are making a strong recovery now that they are protected from these deadly chemicals.

Another insidious form that pollution can take, which has found its way increasingly into the news in recent years, is acid rain.

Fuels burned in factories and vehicles produce clouds of chemicals that react with substances in the air to form acid. These acids then become part of rain and snow— and fall back to earth. In lakes, they poison the microscopic plants, called plankton, that are eaten by fish; this kills the fish as well. On land, the acid rains kill trees and other plants, and some animals as well.

Chemicals called PCBs—poly-chlorinated biphenyls—have begun wreaking havoc in natural ecosystems in recent years. PCBs are used in refrigeration and in insulation. They are deadly. When released into the environment, they remain there, as far as anyone can tell, forever. Animals that ingest PCBs give birth to deformed children. In some cases, they even seem to go insane, violently killing their own offspring. Both fish and birds have fallen victim to PCBs in large numbers.

One of the most terrible of pollutants has only recently been recognized as a menace to wildlife, but it may turn out to be the worst menace of all: discarded plastic. When plastic trash is thrown overboard from ships, or dumped into rivers for disposal, it is commonly ingested by marine wildlife, or creatures such as seals and pelicans become entangled in it.

The *Washington Post* reported the harrowing story of a hawksbill turtle found with a belly full of such cast-off plastic: "The young turtle's gut was a trash bin for strands of plastic rope, a plastic balloon, shards of a hard plastic bottle, plastic beads, part of a plastic comb, a plastic golf tee, a plastic toothpaste cap, a plastic toy wheel, the top of a plastic syringe, plastic baggies and a plastic flower." Needless to say, the turtle was dead.

Plastic fish line of the sort used by commercial fishers is an especially dangerous hazard. Pelicans pick up the plastic strands when they dive for fish, then become trapped when the plastic subsequently snags on the branches of trees. Unless rescued by some human samaritan, the pelican will hang upside down from the tree until it starves.

Baby seals can become trapped in fishing lines or in the small holes of the plastic liners used to hold six-packs of beer together; struggling to get free only pulls the snare more tightly around their necks. This has become a major problem among the colonies of Pribilof fur seals mentioned in the last chapter, where nearly thirty thousand seals die *each year* from plastic entanglement!

ACCIDENTAL KILLS

A popular automobile bumper sticker reads I Brake for Small Animals. Leaving aside the question of whether other drivers actually speed up to run over small animals, this sentiment reflects a growing problem for species that live near large human populations. The modern world, full of fast and deadly machinery, is not a safe place for wild animals to live. When a wild animal wanders out of the wild, even if just to cross a highway, it takes its life into its paws.

Everyone has seen the sad sight of a dead animal lying beside the road, where it has been struck and killed by an automobile. The sight is sadder still when the victim is a member of an endangered species, whose numbers are already dwindling. At least two such species, both based in Florida, are severely endangered by accidents from automobiles.

One of these is the Key deer, which lives in the Florida Keys. As visitors to south Florida know, the Keys are narrow and dominated by a single highway that cuts through the middle of this slender peninsula jutting into the Gulf of Mexico.

As befits an inhabitant of such a physically small environment, the Key deer is a tiny animal, only 2 feet (61 cm) tall, and quite vulnerable to automobile accidents. By 1947 only fifty Key deer survived. Although they have struggled back from the brink in subsequent years, automobile accidents still take a heavy toll. From 1947 to 1971, 590 Key deer were killed by cars, 52 in 1971 alone. Warning signs have long been placed alongside the highway, but whether the signs have greatly reduced the mortality of the deer is hard to say. A more effective tactic has been the placing of reflective discs along the roadside, which presumably warn the deer of the headlights of an oncoming car.

The Florida panther has also fallen victim to the automobile plague. Because only a few of the panthers are known to remain in existence, each kill accounts for a large percentage of the population. In 1981 three panthers were killed by cars, one of them a female pregnant with cubs.

Not all "road kills" occur on the road; motorboats present an increasing problem to wildlife that lives in the water. For instance, the Caribbean manatee, a peaceful, cowlike water creature found in Florida, has suffered greatly from the increasing popularity of the motorboat. Because they float near the surface of the water, out of sight of boaters but not out of reach of propellers, the 2,000-pound (907 kg) manatees are subject to death and injury from accidental collisions in lakes and rivers.

Only about 1,000 manatees remain in Florida, and their numbers are shrinking; as many as 105 have been found dead in a single year. Those that are not killed by motorboats commonly sport gaping scars on their backs from repeated collisions.

In this chapter, we've looked at some of the pressures that are driving species extinct at an ever increasing rate. But is this really something that we should worry about? Sure, species are disappearing at a phenomenal rate, but there are plenty of species on this planet. Out of 10 million existing species, why should it concern us if a million fall by the wayside? There will still be 9 million left. And most of the vanished species will be insects and plants that nobody ever knew existed. Why weep for them?

Indeed. Why should we weep for the extinct species? *That* is the subject of the next chapter.

3
DOES EXTINCTION MAKE A DIFFERENCE?

The dinosaurs became extinct 76 million years ago. Does anyone miss them? In the great scheme of things—or in the smaller scheme of individual human lives—does the extinction of the dinosaurs make any real difference?

Possibly not. It's fun to hear stories about these monstrous reptiles and to see pictures of them in books and museums, but it's probably for the best that the occasional brontosaurus can't wander into our backyards. It might wreak havoc with the rosebushes—or eat the family dog.

Of course, if the dinosaurs had never become extinct, the mammals probably never would have evolved beyond a primitive state—and human beings would not exist. So, in a sense, we owe our very existence to the extinction of the dinosaurs. If they hadn't died out, we wouldn't be here.

But to those species that survived the extinction—our distant mammalian ancestors, for instance—the great dying must have been a terrible time to be alive. If the extinction was the result of some natural disaster—if comets rained down from the sky, or volcanoes thrust up through the earth's crust to change the shape of the land—then it must have been a time of great turmoil, even for those species that survived. And even if the extinction was of a gentler sort, caused by gradual rather than abrupt changes in the environment, the loss of so many species would have created another type of turmoil, as the food chain fell apart and the surviving species scrambled to put it back together again by adapting to the available niches. A mass extinction is a traumatic event in the history of a planet, for the winners in the survival sweepstakes as well as for the losers.

The current mass extinction is not a slow, gentle one. With a predicted species loss of more than one species per hour, it may be the most rapid mass extinction in Earth's history, though it is difficult to time the mass extinctions of the ancient past. And, while earlier extinctions were the result of natural (if occasionally violent) changes in the environment, this extinction is the result of unnatural changes, created by that master inventor of unnatural things, *homo sapiens*. Any way we look at it, this extinction is different from the one that killed off the dinosaurs. So while we may be the direct beneficiaries of the dinosaur's demise, we will not benefit from this extinction. In fact, as we destroy the environment in which we evolved, we may turn out to be one of its victims. Ultimately, human beings may become extinct, too.

Why should we be concerned for endangered species? Perhaps you feel that this question doesn't even need to be asked, that it is obvious that we should use every means at our disposal to save those species that are moving toward extinction, whether they be plants, animals, insects, or whatever. Good for you. Other species have as much right to exist as human beings do, even if their existence does not directly benefit humankind.

But there will always be those who ask, "Why? Why should we take responsibility for the fate of other species, when those species may stand in the way of the human development of the planet?" Such a question will inevitably be asked, and you may find yourself confronted by someone asking such a question. In this chapter, we'll attempt to arm you with some answers. Perhaps, by convincing others of the need to save the endangered plants and wildlife of planet Earth, you can play a role in saving these endangered species from extinction.

WHAT RIGHT DO WE HAVE?

Do human beings have any right to endanger the existence of the other species with which we share this planet? And once we have endangered a species, either deliberately or inadvertently, do we have the right *not* to do everything we can to save that species from extinction?

If the tables were turned, and the human race had been somehow endangered by the inadvertent intervention, say, of intelligent beings from a planet circling Alpha Centauri, would we not expect those beings to help us escape the peril they had placed us in? Certainly we'd be angry if they didn't—and anxious for revenge! If the black-footed ferret could understand the plight that we have placed it in through systematic extermination of prairie dogs, and if it could express its feelings on that matter, it seems likely that it would feel much as we would feel about the hypothetical Alpha Centaurians. It would have a right to expect us to save it from extinction—and to be very angry if we did not.

But the black-footed ferret cannot express its feelings. It is up to us, the human race, to act as advocates for the ferret's position, because we *are* capable of understanding the situation it is in. Of all the creatures that have lived on Earth since the first living molecules formed in the primeval seas, only we have the ability to foresee extinctions—and to prevent them. Unfortunately, we also have the ability to *cause* extinctions. Whether we like it or not, we have been given a special responsibility to intervene in the fate of other species, to the extent that such an intervention is in our power.

At least, that is one of the arguments in favor of our taking a role in the saving of endangered species. But it is also possible to argue that the direct interests of the human race, in developing new lands for farming, manufacturing, and sheltering members of the human race, take precedence over the survival of other species. And this is not an easy argument to counter. The human race is growing, and as it grows it needs land and other resources for its survival. At some point, it becomes necessary to balance the needs of the human race against the needs of other species. When the interests of an endangered species conflict with the interests of human beings— as they frequently do—whose interests should take precedence?

This is a thorny question, but it might not be as difficult to answer as it sounds. In a very real way, the interests of the endangered species *are* the interests of humankind, and thus cannot conflict with those interests. The other species of planet Earth are part of the ecosystem in which human beings have evolved, and, in a very real way, we are unable to survive without them. We receive direct benefits from the existence of these species, quite apart from the aesthetic benefits cited above, benefits that we may be evolutionarily incapable of living without.

What are these benefits? Let's look at a few of them.

FOR WHOM THE BELL TOLLS

Each year, millions of visitors flock to the National Zoo in Washington, D.C., to see Hsing-Hsing and Ling-Ling, the giant pandas given to the United States as a gift by the People's Republic of China. In most cases, these visitors don't come to the Panda House because they feel an obligation to support an endangered species—and, even if they did, the support would be purely moral, since there's no charge for visiting the Panda House—but because they simply want to see the pandas. Pandas are a charming and charismatic species, engaging to watch and to study. Most people would agree that this is a better world because it has pandas in it, and that the world would be somehow diminished if pandas ceased to exist.

This is the aesthetic argument for protecting endangered species, the argument for beauty and charm. The world is enriched by a variety of species, and impoverished each time a species dies. We are the poorer for not having passenger pigeons, quaggas, and even dodo birds in our environment. Future generations will be poorer still as one species after another vanishes into an evolutionary sinkhole. Every time we allow a species to become extinct, we cheat ourselves. The seventeenth-century poet John Donne put it this way: "Ask not for whom the [funeral] bell tolls; it tolls for thee."

The problem with the aesthetic argument is that it tends to support the protection of glamorous species, such as the panda, the tiger, or the elephant, at the expense of the unglamorous endangered species, such as the troglodyte shrimp or the thousands of unnamed plants in the equatorial rain forests. What do we lose if a tiny flower in Brazil that no one has ever seen anyway dies without offspring? Is the world poorer for such a loss?

Quite possibly, the answer is yes. But to explain why, we must look at the other benefits that the human race receives from nonhuman species, benefits that go far beyond the aesthetic.

DIRECT BENEFITS

Human beings could not survive on this planet without other species. That's a pretty obvious statement, but sometimes we forget how true it is. Because human beings

exist at a pretty high level on the food chain, we need other species to provide food for our dinner tables. Being omnivores—that is, creatures that eat meat *and* vegetables—we eat both plants, which trap the sun's energy in carbohydrates, and animals, which in turn eat the plants that trap the sun's energy.

Roughly ten thousand years ago, in recognition of the need for maintaining other species as a source of nourishment, human beings discovered agriculture. Agriculture is the deliberate cultivation and domestication of plants and animals to guarantee a perpetual supply for the human dinner table. So far, no domesticated species of either plant or animal has found its way onto the lists of endangered species, because humanity long ago learned to protect its self-interests in this area. However, as we shall see later in this chapter, even cultivated sources of food can be threatened if wild, uncultivated sources are allowed to die away.

Food, however, is by no means the only benefit we receive from our fellow denizens of planet Earth. The oxygen that we breathe, for instance, is produced in the exhalations of plants, mostly in the oceans; these plants also perform the service of cleansing from the atmosphere the carbon dioxide that we (and our factories and vehicles) exhale, before it can reach levels that would be poisonous to us, or that would alter the climate of the planet.

Plants also protect our landscape from wear and tear. Grass and trees on a hillside protect the hillside from erosion. When natural ground covers are removed, the result is often wholesale destruction of the landscape by wind and rain.

*The giant panda
hovers on the verge
of extinction.*

But these are obvious benefits that we receive from other species. There are also less obvious benefits that we receive from nature, benefits that the average person may not be aware of until they are taken away by extinction.

MEDICINE

Herbal remedies for illness—that is, remedies derived from wild or cultivated plants—may be as old as the human race, or older. The medicine man with his bag of herbs is a familiar figure from pre-civilized society, and though we may laugh at those who believe that medicine can be found in places other than a drugstore prescription counter, such laughter would be misguided, because much of the medicine purchased at the prescription counter comes originally from plants found in the wild. Though modern medicine has performed miracles in its conquest of disease, the ancient medicine men knew some things about curing disease that modern scientists are just now discovering.

Roughly one-fourth of all medicines prescribed in the United States are derived in some fashion from plants. The chemicals used in these medicines come from only forty-one different plants, but without these plants modern medicine would be severely crippled. The opium poppy, for instance, supplies such painkillers as codeine and morphine; plants of the genus *Strychnos* are the source of strychnine and curare, which are not just deadly poisons but important muscle relaxants used in surgery; the wild foxglove plant is the source of digitalis, a medicine used in the treatment of heart ailments.

Although such plants can be found in any tropical rain forest, Madagascar has proven to be a particularly fertile source of plants with medicinal value. *Haronga madagascariensis*, a plant that—as its name implies—is unique to Madagascar, is the source of a stomach medicine called *harunganin*. The Madagascan weed *Centella asiatic*

Left: *The rosy periwinkle of Madagascar produces a chemical proven effective in treating some cancers.* Below left: *Foxglove is the source of digitalis, used in the treatment of heart ailments.* Below right: *The opium poppy is the source of such painkillers as codeine and morphine.*

produces a chemical used in a medicine called *Madecassol*, which facilitates the healing of wounds. Another native plant of Madagascar may prove to be the source of a medicine for fighting that ancient but persistent enemy of humankind, the bubonic plague.

Ironically, the usefulness of plants in medicine is a side effect of the adaptations these plants have made to survive in their environments. To protect themselves against predators, many plants have evolved genes for molecules that are poisonous to animals that eat them; these poisonous molecules cause chemical changes to take place in the animals' bodies. When used in a controlled manner, these chemical changes can be useful. For instance, they can destroy the tumors created by cancer, or promote relaxation.

New medical uses for wild plants are being found all the time. The rosy periwinkle plant of Madagascar—yet another Madagascan plant of incalculable medical value—produces a chemical called *vincristine*, which has proven effective in treating several varieties of cancer, including childhood leukemia. Although the rosy periwinkle has long been used in herbal treatments among the Madagascan natives, it is only in recent years that scientists have acknowledged its powers. In the last chapter, we saw that the native wildlife of Madagascar is disappearing at a frightening pace; if the capabilities of the periwinkle had not been recognized in time, it might have become extinct, and the cancer treatments that utilize it never have been developed.

Animals can also be the source of medically valuable chemicals. Snakes produce deadly venoms that, like the poisonous molecules secreted by plants, have medical importance when used in a controlled fashion. Venom from a deadly snake called the Malayan pit viper prevents life-threatening clots from forming in human blood, venom from bee stings can ease the pain of arthritis, and poisons from sea anemones are useful in the fight against cancer.

The curative powers of the rosy periwinkle would not be known today if it weren't for Eli Lilly and Company, the pharmaceuticals manufacturer, which mounted a campaign in the 1950s to find just such plants. How many other plants—and animals—with medicinal value exist in the rain forests of South America and Africa or Madagascar, or the coral reefs of Australia, or in any of a thousand other little-explored regions, that were not found by Lilly, but that may yet be discovered by some other chemical company or scientist, given sufficient time? Possibly thousands, or tens of thousands, yet there is scarcely time to *begin* studying the millions of plants unique to these areas before the rain forests are felled by the ax of those anxious to create lucrative farmland. Every time a species of plant becomes extinct, its potential medical value is lost. Forever.

CHEMICAL FACTORIES

The molecules produced by plants are valuable for more than just medical purposes. A plant is a chemical factory of sorts, and the human race is always finding new uses for chemicals.

Rubber, for instance, comes from plants; in fact, several hundred plants can serve as a source for rubber, though only a few are used commercially. And, of course, rubber has a wide variety of uses.

Alcohol is also derived from plants. Alcohol can be used as fuel, or as a fuel-additive, as an ingredient in beverages, or for medical sterilization.

Plants are also an important source of oil. Of course, the oil that we use in the engines of automobiles comes mostly from plants that died many millions of years ago, but lubricating oils and cooking oils come from plants that grow on Earth today.

As with medicines, it is difficult to say what contributions plants (and animals) may make to the chemical arsenals of the future. And, if we allow the great variety of plants on Earth today to die away, we will never know.

HYBRID VIGOR

We saw in the first chapter how species of plants and animals with small breeding populations come to suffer from inbreeding depression—a condition caused by the expression of too many recessive genes. The cure for inbreeding depression is the introduction of new genes to the gene pool, so that recessive genes are less likely to be received in tandem with identical recessive genes. The introduction of new genes produces *hybrid vigor*, a condition that is the precise opposite of inbreeding depression.

Alas, some of the most valuable species on this planet periodically suffer from inbreeding depression: the plants that we rely on for our daily diet. Surprisingly, considering the vast array of edible plants available in the wild, relatively few are used as food staples for the human race: rice, wheat, and corn are far and away the most popular. Long ago, when *homo sapiens* made the transition from hunter to farmer, these and other species came to be cultivated artificially, so that no one had to rely on the vagaries of wild species for dietary survival.

A cultivated species of a plant is called a *cultivar*; a species that has not been deliberately cultivated is sometimes called a *wild type*. For every cultivar, there is usually a wild type, a relative of the cultivated plant that grows in the wild that no one has attempted to cultivate.

Alas, cultivars commonly fall victim to inbreeding depression because of their relatively small gene pools; thus, some of the most valuable plants on Earth sometimes succumb to genetic weaknesses brought about by an overdose of recessive genes. This is sometimes called *genetic erosion*. Since we rely on these plants for the food on our tables, it is necessary that we have a ready cure at hand for genetic erosion.

The cure lies in the wild-type species. By crossbreeding cultivars with their wild-type relatives, new genes are brought into the gene pool, and hybrid vigor results. The plants are brought back to health.

But what if no wild type of a species existed? What if only the cultivars were left on a planet increasingly plagued by extinctions? The answer is obvious: without the wild type, the cultivated type, too, would eventually become extinct. If enough cultivars became extinct—and it wouldn't take very many—mass famine would be the result. It is necessary, therefore, that we protect the wild types from extinction.

But how? Wild types can't be cultivated; if they were, they would cease to be wild types, and would ultimately be subject to the same genetic erosion that threatens the cultivars. To keep the wild types in existence, we must preserve their habitats—the forests and jungles of Earth, the very environments that are even now being destroyed.

THE GENETIC LIBRARY

We can encapsulate much of what has been said above in two words: genetic library. The millions of species that live on this planet carry within their chromosomes a vast genetic library, a set of irreplaceable recipes for molecules that may have considerable value for the human race. And no two species—or even two members of the same species—carry the same set of recipes. Every time a species becomes extinct, it takes its library of genes with it; the important information in that library is gone.

In some cases, of course, that information might have proved useless even if we had had the opportunity to tap it. But even if the information were useless now, who knows what genetic information the future might require? New diseases will require new cures; new problems will require new chemical solutions. But the plant that carries the chemical or the cure may not exist by the time the problem comes along.

Perhaps someday we will be able to read the genetic information from a plant or animal into a powerful computer which can store that information for the rest of time. And perhaps we will even develop a method of reconstituting those genes and recreating the chemicals that they contain recipes for, perhaps even reconstituting the original plant or animal of which the information was once a part. Then we will no longer need to fear extinction; the genetic library will be safely stored in computer memories or on magnetic diskettes, where disaster is less likely to overtake it. (Of course, entire species may then be wiped out by a single power failure. . . .)

But that day is far in the future. We are not even *close* to having such capabilities today. They are centuries in the future.

For now it is of paramount importance that we protect Earth's vast genetic library by preserving the librarians who guard that information: the species themselves.

4

CAN WE STOP THE EXTINCTIONS?

The problem behind the twentieth century mass extinctions is sometimes referred to as the "tragedy of the commons." A commons is a field used for grazing animals, such as sheep, held in "common" by several herders. No one owns the commons; it is everyone's property.

It is in the interest of every herder to graze as many sheep as possible on the commons. The more sheep each herder grazes, the more profit he or she makes when those sheep are sold for meat and wool. The commons can support only so many sheep at one time. No one herder is likely to graze more sheep on the commons than the commons is able to feed, but if too many sheep are grazed at one time by *all the herders*, the commons will become overgrazed, and the sheep will starve.

When it becomes obvious that the commons is about to be overgrazed, will each herder voluntarily cut down the number of sheep that he or she grazes, voluntarily foregoing individual profit in order to save the commons for all? Not likely. Since no one herder is entirely responsible for the overgrazing, each can rationalize that it is someone else's responsibility to save the commons. And each herder knows that if he or she cuts back on the number of sheep grazed, some other selfish herder will graze *more* sheep and reap extra profits.

As a result, the commons becomes overgrazed and all of the herders suffer.

The natural resources of Earth—the rain forests, the lakes, the oceans, even the endangered species themselves—are a kind of commons: they are the common property of all humankind. No one person, or even a single corporation, can destroy this property. But, collectively, the billions of people on this planet have placed a heavy burden on this common property, a burden that it cannot support. Eventually, these resources will be gone—and it will be the other species of this planet that suffer first. But when those species are gone, humanity will suffer as well, because those other species are part of the environment in which we have evolved, part of the ecosystem for which we are adapted. Humanity cannot survive on this planet alone. Like the herders who destroy the commons, we will bring about our own downfall by overstraining the resources of Earth; the ultimate endangered species may actually be *homo sapiens.*

How can we go about saving this common property? Do we appeal to the charity of humankind, asking each individual to forego self interest—the desire for cheap hamburgers, the desire for more land—in the common interests of all? Is this likely to have more effect than asking the herders not to overgraze the commons?

Maybe it will. Maybe we can convince people that they must stop encroaching on the resources needed by the other species of the planet.

And, then again, maybe not. If past experience is any guide, more than just an appeal to common sense may be required. Traditionally, when common sense has failed to stop people from acting destructively in their own self-interest, it has been necessary to pass laws. Fortunately, laws have already been passed to save endangered species and protect this common resource for all. In the United States, the most important of these laws is the Endangered Species Act of 1973.

THE ENDANGERED SPECIES ACT

The Endangered Species Act prohibits trade in species that have been designated as endangered, that is, in danger of extinction. The job of designating which species are endangered falls to the U.S. Fish and Wildlife Service (FWS), a branch of the U.S. Department of the Interior. The FWS regularly publishes a list in booklet form, *Endangered and Threatened Wildlife and Plants*; a copy of the most recent can be found at the end of this book. The list is compiled on the basis of current scientific evidence. As its name implies, the list contains not only those species regarded as endangered, but those regarded as *threatened*—that is, in danger of becoming endangered.

The act provides penalties for anyone who sells an endangered species or a product made from the body of an endangered species, or who transports an endangered species product between states or between countries. (Exceptions to the act can be granted, however.) In addition, the act makes it illegal for an endangered species to be "killed, hunted, collected, harassed, harmed, pursued, shot, trapped, wounded, or captured."

The list also designates a *critical habitat* for some species. This is the area that the species needs in order to survive; no federal agency may engage in a project that threatens the critical habitat of an endangered species. Unfortunately, this restriction does not apply to private endeavors.

Many states in the United States have laws that complement and enhance the Endangered Species Act.

CONVENTION ON INTERNATIONAL TRADE IN ENDANGERED SPECIES OF WILD FAUNA AND FLORA

Usually abbreviated as CITES, the Convention on International Trade in Endangered Species of Wild Fauna and Flora is the jawbreaking name of the single most important piece of international legislation yet created for the protection of endangered species. CITES, a treaty devised by the International Union for the Conservation of Nature and Natural Resources (IUCN), was ratified in 1975. It regulates international trade in endangered species products. By the mid-1980s, more than eighty nations had signed this treaty.

The endangered species themselves are listed in the appendices to CITES. Appendix I lists species in which trade is absolutely prohibited, except under very special circumstances; these are the species in immediate danger of extinction. Appendices II and III list species for which special export permits must be acquired before trade is authorized.

Unfortunately, there is a loophole in CITES, doubtlessly placed there to facilitate its ratification by a large number of countries. Any nation may take a "reservation" on a species, thereby exempting itself from the restrictions concerning that species. Japan alone has taken reservations on such endangered and threatened species as the fin whale, the hawksbill turtle, and the saltwater crocodile, among others.

The IUCN also publishes the Red Data Books, comprehensive listings of endangered and threatened species around the world. Each entry in the Red Data Books contains valuable data about an endangered species of plant or animal, detailing its habitat, its life-style, its degree of endangerment.

ENFORCING THE LAWS

The existence of laws is not always enough. In order to save endangered species, the laws protecting those species must be enforced rigorously, and exceptions should be made only when they are absolutely unavoidable. Alas, the enforcement of such laws as the Endangered Species Act sometimes leaves something to be desired. A prime example is the case of the snail darter and the Tellico Dam.

For a species that was not even known to science prior to 1973, the snail darter became famous with remarkable speed. By the late 1970s, this tiny, 3-inch-long (8-cm) fish was making headlines in newspapers around the world. What did the snail darter do to deserve such notoriety? It prevented, at least temporarily, the construction of a $120 million dam.

The Tellico Dam Project was initiated in the late 1960s by the Tennessee Valley Authority (TVA). The dam was to be placed on the Little Tennessee River in eastern Tennessee, where it would flood a large valley and create a lake, which would subsequently be used for boating and other recreation. The dam itself would produce electric power for the region.

The fly in the ointment for the Tellico Dam was uncovered in 1973 by a University of Tennessee biologist named David Etnier. While studying the aquatic life of the Little Tennessee River, Etnier discovered a previously unknown species of fish that he called a snail darter, which existed in only a small portion of the river that would be flooded by the dam. Thus, the flooding would destroy the snail darter's habitat—and therefore would bring about the extinction of the snail darter.

The TVA had already been sued by an environmental group, the Environmental Defense Fund, to justify the environmental impact that the dam was expected to have

The tiny snail darter blocked completion of the multimillion-dollar Tellico Dam in Tennessee for about a year. But in the end the Tellico Dam Project was exempt from compliance with the Endangered Species Act, and the snail darter's habitat was destroyed.

on the region. Just as the TVA had filed an environmental impact statement and proceeded with work on the dam, Etnier's discovery was brought to their attention. Needless to say, they were not thrilled with the notion that construction on the dam should be halted to save a single endangered species of fish.

But the Endangered Species Act had just been passed by Congress, and it provided the wedge environmentalists needed to save the snail darter. By 1978, the snail darter had been declared an endangered species, and the TVA was ordered to stop construction by no less a body than the United States Supreme Court. Certainly this was a triumph for those who sided with the rights of endangered species.

The TVA, however, fought back. There was considerable sympathy on its side, in the government and elsewhere. In 1979, a bill was passed by Congress specifically exempting the Tellico Dam from compliance with the Endangered Species Act. The dam was built, the valley flooded—and the habitat of the snail darter destroyed.

Before the species could become extinct, however, it was transplanted by environmentalists to other, similar rivers where it might be able to survive. No one knows what the long-term fate of the snail darter will be, however.

In the case of the snail darter, the letter of the Endangered Species Act was obeyed, while the spirit was violated. No law was broken by the Tellico Dam Project, but a species was deliberately and knowingly endangered, a precedent that should cause concern to anyone worried for the future of endangered species.

LAST-MINUTE RESCUES

Whether or not the spirit of laws designed to protect endangered species is properly enforced may determine the fate of many species other than the snail darter. But even with laws to protect the endangered, the situation for some species is so perilous that only deliberate rescue efforts will save them from extinction. Alas, it is *already* too late to rescue the majority of species teetering on the brink of extinction.

Fortunately, there are many concerned conservationists in this country and elsewhere willing to give of their time and money to help save those species that still might be saved. However, there is some question as to what methods should be used. Consider the case of the California condor.

The natural habitat of the California condor lies along the Pacific Coast of North America, not just in California but from Canada in the north to Mexico in the south. These large birds are carrion eaters—that is, they feed on the carcasses of dead animals. They nest in caves or alongside rocky cliffs. They have never been common, but in recent decades their numbers have fallen precipitously. In the 1940s there were perhaps one hundred of the condors throughout their range, by the early 1960s half that many, and in the late 1970s no more than thirty.

The condors' problem is essentially twofold. Their habitat vanished as humans encroached on their territory. (Some ranchers have even shot and killed the condors, in the mistaken belief that they are killers of livestock, which they are not.) But the condors' natural reproduction rate is also quite slow: they do not begin reproducing until at least the age of six, sometimes even later. A mated pair of condors produces, at most, one egg a year, though sometimes a second egg will be laid if the first comes to harm. Under pressure from the loss of habitat, the birds simply were unable to reproduce quickly enough to replace their own diminishing numbers. (The effect of DDT on the condors' eggs had some impact as well, in the years before that substance was controlled.)

Something clearly had to be done, but what? While

conservationists agree on the necessity for action, they have had trouble agreeing on what that action should be. Essentially, there are two schools of thought on the matter. One believes that the condors must be saved in the wild, in their own habitat. The other believes that the condors must be brought into zoos and other protected habitats and that new generations of condors must be raised there, *then* released into the wild. The dispute between these two groups has been bitter.

One of the central tenets of conservationism is that an endangered species has not been truly saved unless it continues to exist in the wild. No one argues this point. However, there is considerable argument as to whether a new generation of condors raised in zoos would be capable of returning to the wild and surviving there as their ancestors did. Further, there is some doubt that this sort of direct human intervention is good for the condor at all.

On one side of this argument stands the U.S. Fish and Wildlife Service and the National Audubon Society; these organizations proposed a program of *captive breeding* to save the California condor; that is, the wild condors would be captured, taken to zoos and bred; then they and their offspring would be re-released into their natural habitat. On the other side of the argument are such organizations as the Sierra Club and Friends of the Earth, which advocate a "hands-off" policy in the belief that captive breeding would be more destructive than constructive for the species.

The argument came to a head in 1980 when a baby condor died in the hands of a Fish and Wildlife biologist; those who had been staunchly opposed to captive breeding

*By the end of 1986, only
two California condors
remained in the wild.*

maintained that the death would have been avoided had the FWS maintained a hands-off policy.

Soon, however, the issue became moot. In the mid-1980s, the wild condors died at a dizzying rate, and by December 1986, only two California condors remained in the wild; the others had been placed in zoos for captive breeding, under the watchful eye of those who wonder if the species can survive to see the end of the decade.

The story of the California condor is not a cheering one. The story of the whooping crane, on the other hand, though still without a satisfactory ending, is somewhat more upbeat.

For some time the whooper, as it is known to those who have fought for its survival, has been a symbol of endangered species, probably because it was the first endangered species in North America to receive wide public attention, in the late 1930s.

By some estimates, the population of these 6-foot-tall (2-m) birds fell from about fourteen hundred at the time of the discovery of America to twenty-one in the year 1941. Why? In large part, it is a familiar story: the whooper has always been very particular about its habitat, and that habitat has disappeared with the rapid encroachment of humanity. Furthermore, as it makes the long flight from its wintering grounds in the United States to its nesting grounds in Canada, it is a tempting target for the guns of hunters.

The 6-foot (2-m)-tall whooping crane, photographed at Patuxent, Maryland, Wildlife Reserve. In 1941 there were only twenty-one whoopers. Through the efforts of conservationists, there are now more than a hundred.

The wintering grounds on the Texas Gulf Coast were made into a national wildlife refuge in 1937: the Arkansas National Wildlife Refuge. The summer nesting grounds of the whooper were not even known until the mid-1950s; fortunately, they turned out to be in the Wood Buffalo National Park of Canada. Protected by law and by the sheltered environment of the wildlife refuges, the whooper struggled back from the edge of extinction. Today there are more than one hundred whoopers, still not a large population, but at least the numbers are headed in the right direction.

THE LAST REFUGE

Similar stories have happened again and again in the fight to save species from extinction. But despite individual successes, the overall fight to save endangered species has about it a hopeless air, as the natural habitats of Earth are slowly destroyed by the planet's burgeoning human population. By the middle of the twenty-first century, there may be no truly natural habitats left. The rain forests will have fallen, the wetlands paved over. Where will the other species of Earth live when we have destroyed their natural homes?

That is not an easy question to answer. Wildlife refuges are one solution. These are areas set aside by law as habitats for wild species; they may not be plowed under to create farmland or shopping centers. Private organizations have even been formed to buy up land for use as wildlife refuges.

Several African nations have taken the lead in this endeavor. Since the turn of the century, large portions of the African landscape have been set aside as wildlife refuges for a wide range of species.

But there is a limit to how much territory can be set aside for such purposes. And there are already pressures from many quarters to use portions of these refuges, particularly in Africa, for raising food—which would destroy their usefulness for protecting endangered species. In time, civilization may encroach on even the wildlife refuges.

What then is the answer? Some observers believe that the last refuge that will save wild species from extinction when their habitat is gone are the zoos of the world. Originally conceived as profit-making showcases where bizarre (and often maltreated) animals could be exhibited to gawking tourists, zoos have metamorphosed in recent decades into scientific havens where rare and threatened species can be studied and even protected from the forces that are destroying their brethren in the wild. Eventually, the only "wild" animals on Earth may be captives in zoos.

This goes against one of the primary tenets of wildlife conservation, as illustrated by the California condor controversy. But just as the wild population of California condors was eliminated by natural (and not so natural) pressures until only those in the zoos remained, so the pressures of the modern world may eventually make it unfeasible for *any* wildlife to remain in the wild. This horrible and unthinkable fate may someday become very thinkable indeed.

But the capacity of the zoos is limited. Only a few hundred species could be preserved in the world's zoos, a minuscule fraction of those that would become extinct if the habitats of the world are destroyed completely. And the dangers of inbreeding depression would be great. Even now, animals must be carefully swapped about from zoo to zoo to prevent the gene pool of a captive species from becoming too small. When the population of any species passes below a certain size—and this would almost certainly happen to species that survived only in the zoos— genetic erosion would be the eventual, unavoidable fate.

In programs of captive breeding, zoos already play an important role in preparing endangered species for return to the wild. We can hope that the day never comes when there is no wild to which the species can return.

Certainly it is too late to save many of the species that are now approaching extinction. In fact, in many instances there is probably no point in conservationists' wasting their precious resources on species that have no chance of surviving even with their aid. Therefore, the decision must occasionally be made to let a species become extinct because no effort to save it can possibly be enough, or because the effort would best be applied to a species with a greater chance of survival.

An important technique for choosing who will be allowed to die and who will be allowed to survive is called *triage*. The term comes from World War I, when medics would need to decide which dying soldiers on the battlefield should receive the limited medical attention that was available. The wounded soldiers were divided into three groups: those who would survive with or without medical help, those who would die with or without medical help, and those who might survive with medical help but who would probably die without it. Only the third group, those who would benefit most from medical help, received treatment. Those who would die anyway were allowed to die. Those who would live anyway were left to forage for themselves.

Triage is cruel but sometimes necessary. It allowed the medics to concentrate their efforts where they were needed most and to save the largest numbers of the wounded. A kind of triage might be exercised in saving the endangered species of the world. It may be necessary to allow the most hopeless of the endangered to pass into extinction, so as not to diffuse the efforts and the funds available to save the rest.

But who will make the decision? Who will say that the California condor must be abandoned in order to save the whooping crane? Or that the black-footed ferret must be abandoned in favor of the gray wolf? And who will decide if the fate of an animal is more valuable than that of a plant? Or if a mammal should be saved over a fish or a bird?

How wonderful it would be if all the vanishing animals and plants of the world could be saved, but it looks as though that may no longer be possible. The destruction of wildlife and of habitat has gone on for too long. It can be reversed if we work hard enough, but for many species it is too late.

The great dying has already begun.

BIBLIOGRAPHY

Ayensu, Edward S., et. al. *Our Green and Living World.* Washington, D.C.: Smithsonian Institution Press, 1984. A sumptuously produced look at the endangered species of the plant world.

Cadieux, Charles. *These Are the Endangered.* Washington, D.C.: Stone Wall Press, 1981. An illustrated reference to those species currently in danger of extinction.

Day, David. *The Doomsday Book of Animals: A Natural History of Vanished Species.* New York: Viking, 1981. A lavishly illustrated reference book listing most species that have become extinct in the last three-and-a-half centuries.

Durrell, Lee. *State of the Ark: An Atlas of Conservation in Action.* New York: Doubleday, 1986. An illustrated overview of the conservation movement in the mid-1980s, with an emphasis on endangered species.

Ehrlich, Paul. *The Machinery of Nature.* New York: Simon & Schuster, 1986. An introduction to ecology by one of the leading experts in the field.

Ehrlich, Paul and Anne. *Extinction: The Causes and Consequences of the Disappearance of Species*. New York: Random House, 1981. An authoritative look at the reasons why species become extinct.

Luard, Nicholas. *The Wildlife Parks of Africa*. Salem, N.H.: Salem House, 1985. A well-written history of animal refuges on the African continent; includes a list of all major refuges with detailed descriptions.

Nilsson, Greta. *The Endangered Species Handbook*. Washington, D.C.: Animal Welfare Institute, 1983. A thorough overview of the endangered species problem, available for five dollars (1986 price) from the Animal Welfare Institute, P.O. Box 3650, Washington, D.C. 20007.

Tongren, Sally. *To Keep Them Alive: Wild Animal Breeding*. New York: Dembner Books, 1985. A look at the role zoos play in saving endangered animals.

APPENDIX 1
ENDANGERED AND
THREATENED WILDLIFE

Species		Historic range	Status*
Common name	Scientific name		
MAMMALS			
Anoa, lowland	*Bubalus depressicornis* (= *B. anoa depressicornis*).	Indonesia	E
Anoa, mountain	*Bubalus quaresi* (= *B. anoa quaresi*)	.... do	E
Antelope, giant sable	*Hippotragus niger variani*	Angola	E
Argali	*Ovis ammon hodgsoni*	China (Tibet, Himalayas)	E
Armadillo, giant	*Priodontes maximus* (= *giganteus*)	Venezuela and Guyana to Argentina	E
Armadillo, pink fairy	*Chlamyphorus truncatus*	Argentina	E
Ass, African wild	*Equus asinus* (= *africanus*)	Somalia, Sudan, Ethiopia.	E
Ass, Asian wild (= kulan, onager)	*Equus hemionus*	Southwestern and Central Asia....	E
Avahi	*Avahi* (= *Lichanotus*) *laniger* (= entire genus).	Malagasy Republic (= Madagascar)	E
Aye-Aye	*Daubentonia madagascariensis*	Malagasy Republic (= Madagascar)	E
Babirusa	*Babyrousa babyrussa*	Indonesia	E
Baboon, gelada	*Theropithecus gelada*	Ethiopia	T
Bandicoot, barred	*Perameles bougainville*	Australia	E
Bandicoot, desert	*Perameles eremiana*	.... do	E
Bandicoot, lesser rabbit	*Macrotis leucura*	.... do	E
Bandicoot, pig-footed	*Chaeropus ecaudatus*	.... do	E
Bandicoot, rabbit	*Macrotis lagotis*	.... do	E
Banteng	*Bos javanicus* (= *banteng*)	Southeast Asia	E
Bat, Bulmer's fruit (flying fox)	*Aproteles bulmerae*	Papua New Guinea	E
Bat, bumblebee	*Craseonycteris thongiongyai*	Thailand	E
Bat, gray	*Myotis grisescens*	Central and Southeastern U.S.A.	E
Bat, Hawaiian hoary	*Lasiurus cinereus semotus*	U.S.A. (HI)	E
Bat, Indiana	*Myotis sodalis*	Eastern and Midwestern U.S.A.	E
Bat, little Mariana fruit	*Pteropus tokudae*	Western Pacific Ocean: U.S.A. (Guam).	E
Bat, Mariana fruit	*Pteropus mariannus mariannus*.......	Western Pacific Ocean: U.S.A. (Guam, Rota, Tinian, Saipan, Agiguan).	E
Bat, Ozark big-eared	*Plecotus townsendii ingens*	U.S.A. (MO, OK, AR)	E

Common name	Scientific name	Location	Status
Bat, Rodrigues fruit (flying fox)	*Pteropus rodricensis*	Indian Ocean: Rodrigues Island	E
Bat, Singapore roundleaf horseshoe	*Hipposideros ridleyi*	Malaysia	E
Bat, Virginia big-eared	*Plecotus townsendii virginianus*	U.S.A. (KY, WV, VA)	E
Bear, brown	*Ursus arctos pruinosus*	China (Tibet)	E
Bear, brown	*Ursus arctos arctos*	Palearctic	T
Bear, brown or grizzly	*Ursus arctos* (= *U.a. horribilis*)	Holarctic	E
Bear, brown or grizzly	*Ursus arctos* (= *U.a. nelsoni*)	Holarctic	E
Beaver	*Castor fiber birulai*	Mongolia	E
Bison, wood	*Bison bison athabascae*	Canada, Northwesten U.S.A.	E
Bobcat	*Felis rufus escuinapae*	Central Mexico	E
Bontebok (antelope)	*Damaliscus dorcas dorcas*	South Africa	E
Camel, Bactrian	*Camelus bactrianus* (= *ferus*)	Mongolia, China	E
Caribou, woodland	*Rangifer tarandus caribou*	Canada, U.S.A. (AK, ID, ME, MI, MN, MT, NH, VT, WA, WI)	E
Cat, Andean	*Felis jacobita*	Chile, Peru, Bolivia, Argentina	E
Cat, black-footed	*Felis nigripes*	Southern Africa	E
Cat, flat-headed	*Felis planiceps*	Malaysia, Indonesia	E
Cat, Iriomote	*Felis (Mayailurus) iriomotensis*	Japan (Iriomote Island, Ryukyu Islands)	E
Cat, leopard	*Felis bengalensis bengalensis*	India, Southeast Asia	E
Cat, marbled	*Felis marmorata*	Nepal, Southeast Asia, Indonesia	E
Cat, Pakistan sand	*Felis margarita scheffeli*	Pakistan	E
Cat, Temminck's (= golden cat)	*Felis temmincki*	Nepal, China, Southeast Asia, Indonesia (Sumatra)	E
Cat, tiger	*Felis tigrinus*	Costa Rica to northern Argentina	E
Chamois, Apennine	*Rupicapra rupicapra ornata*	Italy	E
Cheetah	*Acinonyx jubatus*	Africa to India	E
Chimpanzee	*Pan troglodytes*	West and Central Africa	T
Chimpanzee, pygmy	*Pan paniscus*	Zaire	T
Chinchilla	*Chinchilla brevicaudata boliviana*	Bolivia	E

—91—

* E: *Endangered*   T: *Threatened*

Note: *"do" is abbreviation of "ditto."*

Source: *Department of the Interior, U.S. Fish and Wildlife Service*

Species		Historic range	Status*
Common name	Scientific name		
MAMMALS			
Civet, Malabar large-spotted	*Viverra megaspila civettina*	India	E
Cochito (= Gulf of California harbor porpoise).	*Phocoena sinus*	Mexico (Gulf of California)	E
Colobus, Preuss's red	*Colobus badius preussi*	Cameroon	E
Cougar, eastern	*Felis concolor couguar*	Eastern North America	E
Deer, Bactrian	*Cervus elaphus bactrianus*	U.S.S.R., Afghanistan	E
Deer, Bawean	*Axis (= Cervus) porcinus kuhli*	Indonesia	E
Deer, Barbary	*Cervus elaphus barbarus*	Morocco, Tunisia, Algeria	E
Deer, Cedros Island Mule	*Odocoileus hemionus cedrosensis*	Mexico (Cedros Island)	E
Deer, Columbian white-tailed	*Odocoileus virginianus leucurus*	U.S.A. (WA, OR)	E
Deer, Corsican red	*Cervus elaphus corsicanus*	Corsica, Sardinia	E
Deer, Eld's brow-antlered	*Cervus eldi*	India to Southeast Asia	E
Deer, Formosan sika	*Cervus nippon taiouanus*	Taiwan	E
Deer, hog	*Axis (= Cervus) porcinus annamiticus*	Thailand, Indochina	E
Deer, key	*Odocoileus virginianus clavium*	U.S.A. (FL)	E
Deer, marsh	*Blastocerus dichotomus*	Argentina, Uruguay, Paraguay, Bolivia, Brazil.	E
Deer, McNeill's	*Cervus elaphus macneilli*	China (Sinkiang, Tibet)	E
Deer, musk	*Moschus spp.* (all species)	Central and East Asia	E
Deer, North China sika	*Cervus nippon mandarinus*	China (Shantung and Chihli Provinces)	E
Deer, pampas	*Ozotoceros bezoarticus*	Brazil, Argentina, Uruguay, Bolivia, Paraguay.	E
Deer, Persian fallow	*Dama dama mesopotamica*	Iraq, Iran	E
Deer, Philippine	*Axis (= Cervus) porcinus calamianensis*	Philippines (Calamian Islands)	E
Deer, Ryukyu sika	*Cervus nippon keramae*	Japan (Ryukyu Islands)	E
Deer, Shansi sika	*Cervus nippon grassianus*	China (Shansi Province)	E
Deer, South China sika	*Cervus nippon kopschi*	Southern China	E
Deer, swamp (= barasingha)	*Cervus duvauceli*	India, Nepal	E
Deer, Yarkand	*Cervus elaphus yarkandensis*	China (Sinkiang)	E
Dhole (= Asiatic wild dog)	*Cuon alpinus*	U.S.S.R., Korea, China, India, Southeast Asia.	E

Common Name	Scientific Name	Distribution	Status
Dibbler	*Antechinus apicalis*	Australia	E
Dog, African wild	*Lycaon pictus*	Sub-Saharan Africa	E
Drill	*Papio leucophaeus*	Equatorial West Africa	E
Dugong	*Dugong dugon*	East Africa to southern Japan, including U.S.A. (Trust Territories).	E
Duiker, Jentink's	*Cephalophus jentinki*	Sierra Leone, Liberia, Ivory Coast	E
Eland, Western Giant	*Taurotragus derbianus derbianus*	Senegal to Ivory Coast	E
Elephant, African	*Loxodonta africana*	Africa	T
Elephant, Asian	*Elephas maximus*	South-central and Southeast Asia	E
Ferret, black-footed	*Mustela nigripes*	Western U.S.A., Western Canada	E
Fox, Northern swift	*Vulpes velox hebes*	U.S.A. (northern plains), Canada	E
Fox, San Joaquin kit	*Vulpes macrotis mutica*	U.S.A. (CA)	E
Fox, Simien	*Canis (Simenia) simensis*	Ethiopia	E
Gazelle, Clark's (=Dibatag)	*Ammodorcas clarkei*	Somalia, Ethiopia	E
Gazelle, Cuvier's	*Gazella cuvieri*	Morocco, Algeria, Tunisia	E
Gazelle, Mhorr	*Gazella dama mhorr*	Morocco	E
Gazelle, Moroccan (=Dorcas)	*Gazella dorcas massaesyla*	Morocco, Algeria, Tunisia	E
Gazelle, Rio de Oro Dama	*Gazella dama lozanoi*	Western Sahara	E
Gazelle, Arabian	*Gazella gazella*	Arabian Peninsula, Palestine, Sinai	E
Gazelle, sand	*Gazella subgutturosa marica*	Jordan, Arabian Peninsula	E
Gazelle, Saudi Arabian	*Gazella dorcas saudiya*	Israel, Iraq, Jordan, Syria, Arabian Peninsula.	E
Gazelle, Pelzein's	*Gazella dorcas pelzelni*	Somalia	E
Gazelle, slender-horned (=Rhim)	*Gazella leptoceros*	Sudan, Egypt, Algeria, Libya	E
Gibbons	*Hylobates* supp. (including *Nomascus*)	China, India, Southeast Asia	E
Goat, wild (=Chitan markhor)	*Capra aegagrus* (=*falconeri chiltanensis*)	Southwestern Asia	E
Goral	*Nemorhaedus goral*	East Asia	E
Gorilla	*Gorilla gorilla*	Central and Western Africa	E
Hare, hispid	*Caprolagus hispidus*	India, Nepal, Bhutan	E
Hartebeest, Swayne's	*Alcelaphus buselaphus swaynei*	Ethiopia, Somalia	E
Hartebeest, Tora	*Alcelaphus buselaphus tora*	Ethiopia, Sudan, Egypt	E
Hog, pygmy	*Sus salvanius*	India, Nepal, Phutan, Sikkim	E
Horse, Przewalski's	*Equus przewalskii*	Mongolia, China	E
Huemul, North Andean	*Hippocamelus antisensis*	Ecuador, Peru, Chine, Bolivia, Argentina.	E

Species		Historic range	Status*
Common name	Scientific name		
MAMMALS			
Huemul, South Andean	*Hippocamelus bisulcus*	Chile, Argentina	E
Hyena, Barbary	*Hyaena hyaena barbara*	Morocco, Algeria, Tunisia	E
Hyena, brown	*Hyaena brunnea*	Southern Africa	E
Ibex, Pyrenean	*Capra pyrenaica pyrenaica*	Spain	E
Ibex, Walia	*Capra walie*	Ethiopia	E
Impala, black-faced	*Aepyceros melampus petersi*	Namibia, Angola	E
Indri	*Indri indri* (= entire genus)	Malagasy Republic (= Madagascar)	E
Jaguar	*Panthera onca*	U.S.A. (TX, NM, AZ), C. and S. America.	E
Jaguarundi	*Felis yagouaroundi cacomitli*	U.S.A. (TX), Mexico	E
Jaguarundi	*Felis yagouaroundi fossata*	Mexico, Nicaragua	E
Jaguarundi	*Felis yagouaroundi panamensis*	Nicaragua, Costa Rica, Panama	E
Jaguarundi	*Felis yagouaroundi tolteca*	U.S.A. (AZ), Mexico	E
Kangaroo, eastern gray	*Macropus giganteus* (all subspecies except *tasmaniensis*).	Australia	T
Kangaroo, red	*Macropus* (*Megaleia*) *rufus*	do	T
Kangaroo, Tasmanian forester	*Macropus giganteus tasmaniensis*	Australia (Tasmania)	E
Kangaroo, western gray	*Macropus fuliginosus*	Australia	T
Kouprey	*Bos sauveli*	Vietnam, Laos, Cambodia, Thailand	E
Langur, capped	*Presbytis pileata*	India, Burma, Bangladesh	E
Langur, entellus	*Presbytis entellus*	China (Tibet), India, Pakistan, Kashmir, Sri Lanka, Sikkim, Bangladesh.	E
Langur, Douc	*Pygathrix nemaeus*	Cambodia, Laos, Vietnam	E
Langur, Francois'	*Presbytis francoisi*	China (Kwangsi), Indochina	E
Langur, golden	*Presbytis geei*	India (Assam), Bhutan	E
Langur, long-tailed	*Presbytis potenziani*	Indonesia	T
Langur, Pagi Island	*Nasalis* (*Simias*) *concolor*	do	E
Langur, purple-faced	*Presbytis senex*	Sri Lanka (= Ceylon)	T
Langur, Tonkin snub-nosed	*Pygathrix* (*Rhinopithecus*) *avunculus*	Vietnam	T
Lechwe, red	*Kobus leche*	Southern Africa	T

Common name	Scientific name	Range	Status
Lemurs	Lemuridae (incl. Cheirogaleidae, Lepilemuridae); all members of genera *Lemur*, *Phaner*, *Hapalemur*, *Lepilemur*, *Microcebus*, *Allocebus*, *Cheirogaleus*, *Varecia*.	Malagasy Republic (= Madagascar)	E
Leopard	*Panthera pardus*	Africa, Asia	E
Leopard, clouded	*Neofelis nebulosa*	Southeast and south-central Asia, Taiwan.	E
Leopard, snow	*Panthera uncia*	Central Asia	E
Linsang, spotted	*Prionodon pardicolor*	Nepal, Assam, Vietnam, Cambodia, Laos, Burma.	E
Lion, Asiatic	*Panthera leo persica*	Turkey to India	E
Loris, lesser slow	*Nycticebus pygmaeus*	Indochina	T
Lynx, Spanish	*Felis (= Lynx) pardina*	Spain, Portugal.	E
Macaque, Formosan rock	*Macaca cyclopis*	Taiwan	T
Macaque, Japanese	*Macaca fuscata*	Japan (Shikoku, Kyushu and Konshu Islands).	T
Macaque, lion-tailed	*Macaca silenus*	India	E
Macaque, stump-tailed	*Macaca arctoides*	India (Assam) to southern China	T
Macaque, Toque	*Macaca sinica*	Sri Lanka (= Ceylon)	T
Manatee, Amazonian	*Trichechus inunguis*	South America (Amazon River Basin)	E
Manatee, West African	*Trichechus senegalensis*	West Coast of Africa from Senegal River to Cuanza River.	T
Manatee, West India (Florida)	*Trichechus manatus*	U.S.A. (southeastern), Caribbean Sea, South America.	E
Mandrill	*Papio sphinx*	Equatorial West Africa	E
Mangabey, Tana River	*Cercocebus galeritus*	Kenya	E
Mangabey, white-collared	*Cercocebus torquatus*	Senegal to Ghana; Nigeria to Gabon	E
Margay	*Felis wiedii*	U.S.A. (TX), C. and S. America	E
Markhor, Kabal	*Capra falconeri megaceros*	Afghanistan, Pakistan	E
Markhor, straight-horned	*Capra falconeri jerdoni*	do	E
Marmoset, buff-headed	*Callithrix flaviceps*	....	E
Marmoset, cotton-top	*Saguinus oedipus*	Costa Rica to Colombia	E
Marmoset, Goeldi's	*Callimico goeldii*	Brazil, Colombia, Ecuador, Peru, Bolivia.	E

Species		Historic range	Status*
Common name	Scientific name		
MAMMALS			
Marmot, Vancouver Island	*Marmota vancouverensis*	Canada (Vancouver Island)	E
Marsupial, eastern jerboa	*Antechinomys laniger*	Australia	E
Marsupial-mouse, large desert	*Sminthopsis psammophila*	do	E
Marsupial-mouse, long-tailed	*Sminthopsis longicaudata*	do	E
Marten, Formosan yellow-throated	*Martes flavigula chrysospila*	Taiwan	E
Monkey, black colobus	*Colobus satanas*	Equatorial Guinea, People's Republic of Congo, Cameroon, Gabon.	E
Monkey, black howler	*Alouatta pigra*	Mexico, Guatemala, Belize	T
Monkey, Diana	*Cercopithecus diana*	Coastal West Africa	E
Monkey, howler	*Alouatta palliata (= villosa)*	Mexico to South America	E
Monkey, L'hoest's	*Cercopithecus lhoesti*	Upper Eastern Congo Basin, Cameroon.	E
Monkey, Preuss' red colobus	*Colobus badius preussi*	Cameroon	E
Monkey, proboscis	*Nasalis larvatus*	Borneo	E
Monkey, red-backed squirrel	*Saimiri oerstedii*	Costa Rica, Panama	E
Monkey, red-bellied	*Cercopithecus erythrogaster*	Western Nigeria	E
Monkey, red-eared nose-spotted	*Cercopithecus erythrotis*	Nigeria, Cameroon, Fernando Po	E
Monkey, spider	*Ateles geoffroyi frontatus*	Costa Rica, Nicaragua	E
Monkey, spider	*Ateles geoffroyi panamensis*	Costa Rica, Panama	E
Monkey, Tana River red colobus	*Colobus rufomitratus (= badius) rufomitratus.*	Kenya	E
Monkey, woolly spider	*Brachyteles arachnoides*	Brazil	E
Monkey, yellow-tailed woolly	*Lagothrix flavicauda*	Andes of northern Peru.	E
Monkey, Zanzibar red colobus	*Colobus kirki*	Tanzania	E
Mouse, Alabama beach	*Peromyscus polionotus ammobates*	U.S.A. (AL)	E
Mouse, Australian native	*Zyzomys (= Notomys) pedunculatus*	Australia	E
Mouse, Australian native	*Notomys aquilo*	do	E
Mouse, Choctawhatchee beach	*Peromyscus polionotus allophrys*	U.S.A. (FL)	E
Mouse, Field's	*Pseudomys fieldi*	Australia	E
Mouse, Gould's	*Pseudomys gouldii*	do	E
Mouse, Key Largo cotton	*Peromyscus gossypinus allapaticola*	U.S.A. (FL)	E

Common name	Scientific name	Range	Status
Mouse, New Holland	*Pseudomys novaehollandiae*	Australia	E
Mouse, Perdido Key beach	*Peromyscus polionotus trissyllepsis*	U.S.A. (AL, FL)	E
Mouse, salt marsh harvest	*Reithrodontomys raviventris*	U.S.A. (CA)	E
Mouse, Shark Bay	*Pseudomys praeconis*	Australia	E
Mouse, Shortridge's	*Pseudomys shortridgei*	......do......	E
Mouse, Smoky	*Pseudomys fumeus*	......do......	E
Mouse, western	*Pseudomys occidentalis*	......do......	E
Muntjac, Fea's	*Muntiacus feae*	Northern Thailand, Burma	E
Native-cat, eastern	*Dasyurus viverrinus*	Australia	E
Numbat	*Myrmecobius fasciatus*	......do......	E
Ocelot	*Felis pardalis*	U.S.A. (AZ,TX) to C. and S. America	E
Orangutan	*Pongo pygmaeus*	Borneo, Sumatra	E
Oryx, Arabian	*Oryx leucoryx*	Arabian Peninsula	E
Otter, Cameroon clawless	*Aonyx (Paraonyx) congica microdon*	Cameroon, Nigeria	E
Otter, giant	*Pteronura brasiliensis*	South America	E
Otter, long-tailed	*Lutra longicaudis* (incl. *platensis*)	......do......	E
Otter, marine	*Lutra felina*	Peru south to Straits of Magellan	E
Otter, southern river	*Lutra provocax*	Chile, Argentina	E
Otter, southern sea	*Enhydra lutris nereis*	West coast U.S.A. (WA, OR, CA) south to Mexico (Baja California).	T
Panda, giant	*Ailuropod melanoleuca*	People's Republic of China	E
Pangolin (= scaly anteater)	*Manis temmincki*	Africa	E
Panther, Florida	*Felis concolor coryi*	U.S.A. (LA and AR east to SC and FL)	E
Planigale, little	*Planigale ingrami subtilissima* (formerly *P. subtilissima*).	Australia	E
Planigale, southern	*Planigale tenuirostris*	......do......	E
Porcupine, thin-spined	*Chaetomys subspinosus*	Brazil	E
Possum, mountain pygmy	*Burramys parvus*	Australia	E
Possum, scaly-tailed	*Wyulda squamicaudata*	......do......	E
Prairie dog, Mexican	*Cynomys mexicanus*	Mexico	E
Prairie dog, Utah	*Cynomys parvidens*	U.S.A. (UT)	T
Pronghorn, peninsular	*Antilocapra americana peninsularis*	Mexico (Baja California)	E
Pronghorn, Sonoran	*Antilocapra americana sonoriensis*	U.S.A. (AZ), Mexico	E
Pudu	*Pudu pudu*	Southern South America	E
Puma, Costa Rican	*Felis concolor costaricensis*	Nicaragua, Panama, Costa Rica	E

—97—

Species		Historic range	Status*
Common name	Scientific name		
MAMMALS			
Quokka..................	*Setonix brachyurus*..........	Australia	E
Rabbit, Ryukyu..........	*Pentalagus furnessi*..........	Japan (Ryukyu Islands)	E
Rabbit, volcano	*Romerolagus diazi*	Mexico	E
Rat, false water	*Xeromys myoides*	Australia	E
Rat, Fresno kangaroo....	*Dipodomys nitratoides exilis*..	U.S.A. (CA)	E
Rat, Morro Bay kangaroo....	*Dipodomys heermanni morroensis*.	.... do......	E
Rat, stick-nest.........	*Leporillus conditor*	Australia	E
Rat-kangaroo, brush-tailed	*Bettongia penicillata*	.... do......	E
Rat-kangaroo, Gaimard's...	*Bettongia gaimardi*........	.... do......	E
Rat-kangaroo, Lesueur's....	*Bettongia lesueur*	.... do......	E
Rat-kangaroo, plain	*Caloprymnus campestris* ...	.... do......	E
Rat-kangaroo, Queensland	*Bettongia tropica*	.... do......	E
Rhinoceros, black	*Diceros bicornis*...........	Sub-Saharan Africa	E
Rhinoceros, great Indian	*Rhinoceros unicornis*	India, Nepal...........	E
Rhinoceros, Javan	*Rhinoceros sondaicus*......	Indonesia, Indochina, Burma, Thailand, Sikkim, Bangladesh, Malaysia.	E
Rhinoceros, northern white	*Ceratotherium simum cottoni*	Zaire, Sudan, Uganda, Central African Republic.	E
Rhinoceros, Sumatran	*Dicerorhinus (= Didermoceros) sumatrensis.*	Bangladesh to Vietnam to Indonesia (Borneo).	E
Saiga, Mongolian (antelope)	*Saiga tatarica mongolica*	Mongolia...........	E
Saki, white-nosed	*Chiropotes albinasus*........	Brazil	E
Seal, Caribbean monk	*Monachus tropicalis*	Caribbean Sea, Gulf of Mexico	E
Seal, Guadalupe fur	*Arctocephalus townsendi*	U.S.A. (Farallon Islands, CA) south to Mexico (Islas Revillagigedo).	T
Seal, Hawaiian monk	*Monachus schauinslandi*	Hawaiian Archipelago	E
Seal, Mediterranean monk	*Monachus monachus*	Mediterranean, Northwest African Coast and Black Sea.	E
Seledang (= Gaur)........	*Bos gaurus*.............	Bangladesh, Southeast Asia, India	E
Serow, Sumatran	*Capricornis sumatraensis*	Sumatra	E

Common name	Scientific name	Location	Status
Serval, Barbary	*Felis serval constantina*	Algeria	E
Shapo	*Ovis vignei vignei*	Kashmir	E
Shou	*Cervus elaphus wallichi*	Tibet, Bhutan	E
Siamang	*Symphalangus syndactylus*	Malaysia, Indonesia	E
Sifakas	*Propithecus* spp. (all species)	Malagasy Republic (= Madagascar)	E
Sloth, Brazilian three-toed	*Bradypus torquatus*	Brazil	E
Solenodon, Cuban	*Solenodon (Atopogale) cubanus*	Cuba	E
Solenodon, Haitian	*Solenodon paradoxus*	Dominican Republic, Haiti	E
Squirrel, Carolina northern flying	*Glaucomys sabrinus coloratus*	U.S.A. (NC, TN)	E
Squirrel, Delmarva Peninsula fox	*Sciurus niger cinereus*	U.S.A. (Delmarva Peninsula to southeast PA)	E
Squirrel, Virginia northern flying	*Glaucomys sabrinus fuscus*	U.S.A. (VA, WV)	E
Stag, Barbary	*Cervus elaphus barbarus*	Tunisia, Algeria	E
Stag, Kashmir	*Cervus elaphus hanglu*	Kashmir	E
Suni, Zanzibar	*Neotragus (Nesotragus) moschatus moschatus*	Zanzibar (and nearby islands)	E
Tahr, Arabian	*Hemitragus jayakari*	Oman	E
Tamaraw	*Bubalus mindorensis*	Philippines	E
Tamarin, golden-rumped (= golden-headed Tamarin; = golden-lion Marmoset)	*Leontopithecus (= Leontideus)* spp. (all species)	Brazil	E
Tamarin, pied	*Saguinus bicolor*	Northern Brazil	E
Tamarin, white-footed	*Saguinus leucopus*	Northern Colombia	T
Tapir, Asian	*Tapirus indicus*	Burma, Laos, Cambodia, Vietnam, Malaysia, Indonesia, Thailand.	E
Tapir, Brazilian	*Tapirus terrestris*	Colombia and Venezuela south to Paraguay and Argentina.	E
Tapir, Central American	*Tapirus bairdii*	Southern Mexico to Colombia and Ecuador.	E
Tapir, mountain	*Tapirus pinchaque*	Colombia, Ecuador and possibly Peru and Venezuela.	E
Tarsier, Philippine	*Tarsius syrichta*	Philippines	T
Tiger	*Panthera tigris*	Temperate and Tropical Asia	E
Tiger, Tasmanian (= Thylacine)	*Thylacinus cynocephalus*	Australia	E
Uakari (all species)	*Cacajao* spp. (all species)	Peru, Brazil, Ecuador, Colombia, Venezuela.	E

Species		Historic range	Status*
Common name	Scientific name		
MAMMALS			
Urial	Ovis musimon (= orientalis) ophion	Cyprus	E
Vicuña	Vicugna vicugna	South America (Andes)	E
Vole, Amargosa	Microtus californicus scirpensis	U.S.A. (CA)	E
Wallaby, banded hare	Lagostrophus fasciatus	Australia	E
Wallaby, brindled nail-tailed	Onychogalea fraenata	do	E
Wallaby, crescent nail-tailed	Onychogalea lunata	do	E
Wallaby, Parma	Macropus parma	do	E
Wallaby, Western hare	Lagorchestes hirsutus	do	E
Wallaby, yellow-footed rock	Petrogale xanthropus	do	E
Whale, blue	Balaenoptera musculus	Oceanic	E
Whale, bowhead	Balaena mysticetus	Oceanic (north latitudes only)	E
Whale, finback	Balaenoptera physalus	Oceanic	E
Whale, gray	Eschrichtius robustus	North Pacific Ocean: coastal and Bering Sea.	E
Whale, humpback	Megaptera novaeangliae	Oceanic	E
Whale, right	Balaena glacialis	do	E
Whale, Sei	Balaenoptera borealis	do	E
Whale, sperm	Physeter catodon	do	E
Wolf, gray	Canis lupus	Holarctic	E
Wolf, maned	Chrysocyon brachyurus	Argentina, Bolivia, Brazil, Paraguay, Uruguay.	E
Wolf, red	Canis rufus	U.S.A. (southeastern U.S.A. west to central TX).	E
Wombat, hairy-nosed (= Barnard's and Queensland hairy-nosed).	Lasiorhinus krefftii (formerly L. barnardi and L. gillespiei).	Australia	E
Woodrat, Key Largo	Neotoma floridana smalli	U.S.A. (FL)	E
Yak, wild	Bos grunniens	China (Tibet), India	E
Zebra, Grevy's	Equus grevyi	Kenya, Ethiopia, Somalia	T
Zebra, Hartmann's mountain	Equus zebra hartmannae	Namibia, Angola	T
Zebra, mountain	Equus zebra zebra	South Africa	E

BIRDS

Common name	Scientific name	Location	Status
Akepa, Hawaii (honeycreeper)	*Loxops coccineus coccineus*	U.S.A. (HI)	E
Akepa, Maui (honeycreeper)	*Loxops coccineus ochraceus*	do	E
Akialoa, Kauai (honeycreeper)	*Hemignathus procerus*	do	E
Akiapolaau (honeycreeper)	*Hemignathus munroi (= wilsoni)*	do	E
Albatross, short-tailed	*Diomedea albatrus*	North Pacific Ocean: Japan, U.S.S.R., U.S.A. (AK, CA, HI, OR, WA).	E
Blackbird, yellow-shouldered	*Agelaius xanthomus*	U.S.A. (PR)	E
Bobwhite, masked (quail)	*Colinus virginianus ridgwayi*	U.S.A. (AZ), Mexico (Sonora)	E
Booby, Abbott's	*Sula abbotti*	Indian Ocean: Christmas Island	E
Bristlebird, western	*Dasyornis brachypterus longirostris*	Australia	E
Bristlebird, western rufous	*Dasyornis broadbenti littoralis*	do	E
Broadbill, Guam	*Myiagra freycineti*	Western Pacific Ocean: U.S.A. (Guam)	E
Bulbul, Mauritius olivaceous	*Hypsipetes borbonicus olivaceus*	Indian Ocean: Mauritius	E
Bullfinch, Sao Miguel (finch)	*Pyrrhula pyrrhula murina*	Eastern Atlantic Ocean: Azores	E
Bushwren, New Zealand	*Xenicus longipes*	New Zealand	E
Bustard, great Indian	*Choriotis nigriceps*	India, Pakistan	E
Cahow (= Bermuda Petrel)	*Pterodroma cahow*	North Atlantic Ocean: Bermuda	E
Condor, Andean	*Vultur gryphus*	Colombia to Chile and Argentina	E
Condor, California	*Gymnogyps californianus*	U.S.A. (OR, CA), Mexico (Baja California).	E
Coot, Hawaiian (= alae keo keo)	*Fulica americana alai*	U.S.A. (HI)	E
Cotinga, banded	*Cotinga maculata*	Brazil	E
Cotinga, white-winged	*Xipholena atropurpurea*	do	E
Crane, black-necked	*Grus nigricollis*	China (Tibet)	E
Crane, Cuba sandhill	*Grus canadensis nesiotes*	West Indies: Cuba	E
Crane, hooded	*Grus monacha*	Japan, U.S.S.R.	E
Crane, Japanese	*Grus japonensis*	China, Japan, Korea, U.S.S.R.	E
Crane, Mississippi sandhill	*Grus canadensis pulla*	U.S.A. (MS)	E
Crane, Siberian white	*Grus leucogeranus*	U.S.S.R. (Siberia) to India, including Iran and China.	E
Crane, white-naped	*Grus vipio*	Mongolia	E
Crane, whooping	*Grus americana*	Canada, U.S.A. (Rocky Mountains east to Carolinas), Mexico.	E

—101—

Species		Historic range	Status*
Common name	Scientific name		
BIRDS			
Creeper, Hawaii	*Oreomystis (= Loxops) mana*	U.S.A.(HI)	E
Creeper, Molokai (= kakawahie)	*Paroreomyza (= Oreomystis, = Loxops) flammea.*	do	E
Creeper, Oahu (= alauwahio)	*Paroreomyza (= Oreomystis, = Loxops) maculata.*	do	E
Crow, Hawaiian (= 'alala)	*Corvus hawaiiensis (= tropicus)*	do	E
Crow, Mariana	*Corvus kubaryi*	Western Pacific Ocean: U.S.A. (Guam, Rota).	E
Cuckoo-shrike, Mauritius	*Coquus (= Coracina) typicus*	Indian Ocean: mauritius	E
Cuckoo-shrike, Reunion	*Coquus (= Coracina) newtoni*	Indian Ocean: Reunion	E
Curassow, razor-billed	*Mitu (= Crax) mitu mitu*	Brazil (Eastern)	E
Curassow, red-billed	*Crax blumenbachii*	Brazil	E
Curassow, Trinidad white-headed	*Pipile pipile pipile*	West Indies: Trinidad	E
Curlew, Eskimo	*Numenius borealis*	Alaska and northern Canada to Argentina.	E
Dove, cloven-feathered	*Drepanoptila holosericea*	Southwest Pacific Ocean: New Caledonia.	E
Dove, Grenada gray-footed	*Leptotila rufaxilla wellsi.*	West Indies: Grenada	E
Duck, Hawaiian (= koloa)	*Anas wyvilliana*	U.S.A. (HI)	E
Duck, Laysan	*Anas laysanensis*	do	E
Duck, pink-headed	*Rhodonessa caryophyllacea*	India	E
Duck, white-winged wood	*Cairina scutulata*	India, Malaysia, Indonesia, Thailand	E
Eagle, Greenland white-tailed	*Haliaeetus albicilla groenlandicus*	Greenland and adjacent Atlantic islands.	E
Eagle, harpy	*Harpia harpyia*	Mexico south to Argentina	E
Eagle, Philippine (= monkey-eating)	*Pithecophaga jefferyi*	Philippines	E
Eagle, bald	*Haliaeetus leucocephalus*	North America south to northern Mexico.	E
Eagle, Spanish imperial	*Aquila heliaca adalberti*	Spain, Morocco, Algeria	E
Egret, Chinese	*Egretta eulophotes*	China, Korea	E

—102—

Common name	Scientific name	Range	Status
Falcon, American peregrine	*Falco peregrinus anatum*	Nests from central Alaska across north-central Canada to central Mexico, winters south to South America.	E
Falcon, Arctic peregrine	*Falco peregrinus tundrius*	Nests from northern Alaska to Greenland; winters south to Central and South America.	T
Falcon, Eurasian peregrine	*Falco peregrinus peregrinus*	Europe, Eurasia south to Africa and Mideast.	E
Falcon, peregrine	*Falco peregrinus*	Worldwide, except Antarctica and most pacific Islands	E
Finch, Laysan (honeycreeper)	*Telespyza (= Psittirostra) cantans*	U.S.A. (HI)	E
Finch, Nihoa (honeycreeper)	*Telespyza (= Psittirostra) ultima*	....do....	E
Flycatcher, Euler's	*Empidonax euleri johnstonei*	West Indies: Grenada	E
Flycatcher, Seychelles paradise	*Terpsiphone corvina*	Indian Ocean: Seychelles	E
Flycatcher, Tahiti	*Pomarea nigra*	South Pacific Ocean: Tahiti	E
Fody, Seychelles (weaver-finch)	*Foudia sechellarum*	Indian Ocean: Seychelles	E
Frigatebird, Andrew's	*Fregata andrewsi*	East Indian Ocean	E
Goose, Aleutian Canada	*Branta canadensis leucopareia*	U.S.A. (AK, CA, OR, WA), Japan	E
Goose, Hawaiian (= nene)	*Nesochen (= Branta) sandvicensis*	U.S.A. (HI)	E
Goshawk, Christmas Island	*Accipiter fasciatus natalis*	Indian Ocean: Christmas Island	E
Grackle, slender-billed	*Quiscalus (= Cassidix) palustris*	Mexico	E
Grasswren, Eyrean (flycatcher)	*Amytornis goyderi*	Australia	E
Grebe, Atitlan	*Podilymbus gigas*	Guatemala	E
Greenshank, Nordmann's	*Tringa guttifer*	U.S.S.R., Japan, south to Malaya, Borneo.	E
Guan, horned	*Oreophasis derbianus*	Guatemala, Mexico.	E
Gull, Audouin's	*Larus audouinii*	Mediterranean Sea	E
Gull, relict	*Larus relictus*	India, China.	E
Hawk, Anjouan Island sparrow	*Accipiter francesii pusillus*	Indian Ocean: Comoro Islands	E
Hawk, Galapagos	*Buteo galapagoensis*	Ecuador (Galapagos Islands).	E
Hawk, Hawaiian (= Io)	*Buteo solitarius*	U.S.A. (HI).	E
Hermit, hook-billed (hummingbird)	*Glaucis (= Ramphodon) dohrnii*	Brazil.	E
Honeycreeper, crested (= 'akohekohe)	*Palmeria dolei*	U.S.A. (HI)	E
Hornbill, helmeted	*Rhinoplax vigil*	Thailand, Malaysia	E

—103—

Species		Historic range	Status*
Common name	Scientific name		
BIRDS			
Honeyeater, helmeted	*Meliphaga cassidix*	Australia	E
Ibis, Japanese crested	*Nipponia nippon*	China, Japan, U.S.S.R., Korea	E
Kagu	*Rhynochetos jabatus*	South Pacific Ocean: New Caledonia	E
Kakapo (= owl-parrot)	*Strigops habroptilus*	New Zealand	E
Kestrel, Mauritius	*Falco punctatus*	Indian Ocean: Mauritius	E
Kestrel, Seychelles	*Falco araea*	Indian Ocean: Seychelles Islands	E
Kingfisher, Guam Micronesian	*Halcyon cinnamomina cinnamomina*	Western Pacific Ocean: U.S.A. (Guam)	E
Kite, Cuba hook-billed	*Chondrohierax uncinatus wilsonii*	West Indies: Cuba	E
Kite, Grenada hook-billed	*Chondrohierax uncinatus mirus*	West Indies: Grenada	E
Kite, Everglade snail	*Rostrhamus sociabilis plumbeis*	U.S.A. (FL)	E
Kokako (wattlebird)	*Callaeas cinerea*	New Zealand	E
Macaw, glaucous	*Anodorhynchus glaucus*	Paraguay, Uruguay, Brazil	E
Macaw, indigo	*Anodorhynchus leari*	Brazil	E
Macaw, little blue	*Cyanopsitta spixii*	do	E
Magpie-robin, Seychelles (thrush)	*Copsychus sechellarum*	Indian ocean: Seychelles Islands	E
Malkoha, red-faced (cuckoo)	*Phaenicophaeus pyrrhocephalus*	Sri Lanka (= Ceylon)	E
Mallard, Mariana	*Anas oustaleti*	West Pacific Ocean: U.S.A. (Guam, Mariana Islands)	E
Megapode, Micronesian (= La Perouse's)	*Megapodius laperouse*	West Pacific Ocean: U.S.A. (Palau Island, Mariana Islands)	E
Megapode, Maleo	*Macrocephalon maleo*	Indonesia (Celebes)	E
Millerbird, Nihoa (old world warbler)	*Acrocephalus familiaris kingi*	U.S.A. (HI)	E
Monarch, Tinian (old world flycatcher)	*Monarcha takatsukasae*	Western Pacific Ocean: U.S.A. (Mariana Islands)	E
Moorhen (= gallinule), Hawaiian common.	*Gallinula chloropus sandvicensis*	U.S.A. (HI)	E
Moorhen (= gallinule), Mariana common.	*Gallinula chloropus guami*	Western Pacific Ocean: U.S.A. (Guam, Tinian, Saipan, Pagan).	E
Nightjar, (= whip-poor-will), Puerto Rico	*Caprimulgus noctitherus*	U.S.A. (PR)	E
Nukupu'u (honeycreeper)	*Hemignathus lucidus*	U.S.A. (HI)	E

'O'o, Kauai (= 'O'o 'A'a) (honeyeater) ..	*Moho braccatus*	.... do	E
Ostrich, Arabian	*Struthio camelus syriacus*	Jordan, Saudi Arabia	E
Ostrich, West African	*Struthio camelus spatzi*	Spanish Sahara	E
'O'u (honeycreeper)	*Psittirostra psittacea*	U.S.A. (HI)	E
Owl, Anjouan scops	*Otus rutilus capnodes*	Indian Ocean: Comoro Island ...	E
Owl, giant scops	*Otus gurneyi*	Philippines: Marinduque and Mindanao Islands.	E
Owl, Seychelles	*Otus insularis*	Indian Ocean: Seychelles Islands ...	E
Owlet, Morden's (= Sokoke)	*Otus ireneae*	Kenya	E
Palila (honeycreeper)	*Loxioides (= Psittirostra) bailleuri*	U.S.A. (HI)	E
Parakeet, Forbes'	*Cyanoramphus auriceps forbesi* ...	New Zealand	E
Parakeet, golden	*Aratinga guarouba*	Brazil	E
Parakeet, golden-shouldered (= hooded).	*Psephotus chrysopterygius* ...	Australia	E
Parakeet, Mauritius	*Psittacula echo*	Indian Ocean: Mauritius	E
Parakeet, ochre-marked	*Pyrrhura cruentata*	Brazil	E
Parakeet, orange-bellied	*Neophema chrysogaster*	Australia	E
Parakeet, paradise (= beautiful)	*Psephotus pulcherrimus*	.... do	E
Parakeet, scarlet-chested (= splendid) ...	*Neophema splendida*	.... do	E
Parakeet, turquoise	*Neophema pulchella*	.... do	E
Parrot, Australian	*Geopsittacus occidentalis*	.... do	E
Parrot, Bahaman or Cuban.............	*Amazona leucocephala*	West Indies: Cuba, Bahamas, Caymans ..	E
Parrot, ground	*Pezoporus wallicus*	Australia	E
Parrot, imperial	*Amazona imperialis*	West Indies: Dominica	E
Parrot, Puerto Rican	*Amazona vittata*	U.S.A. (PR)	E
Parrot, red-browed	*Amazona rhodocorytha*	Brazil	E
Parrot, red-capped....................	*Pionopsitta pileata*	.... do	E
Parrot, red-necked....................	*Amazona arausiaca*	West Indies: Dominica	E
Parrot, red-spectacled	*Amazona pretrei pretrei*	Brazil, Argentina	E
Parrot, St. Lucia	*Amazona versicolor*	West Indies: St. Lucia	E
Parrot, St. Vincent	*Amazona guildingii*	West Indies: St. Vincent	E
Parrot, thick-billed	*Rhynchopsitta pachyrhyncha*	Mexico, U.S.A. (AZ, NM) ...	E
Parrot, vinaceous-breasted	*Amazona vinacea*	Brazil	E
Parrotbill, Maui (honeycreeper)	*Pseudonestor xanthophrys*	U.S.A. (HI)	E

Species		Historic range	Status*
Common name	Scientific name		
BIRDS			
Pelican, brown	*Pelecanus occidentalis*	U.S.A. (Carolinas to TX, CA), West Indies, C. and S. America: Coastal.	E
Penguin, Galapagos	*Spheniscus mendiculus*	Ecuador (Galapagos Islands).	E
Petrel, Hawaiian dark-rumped	*Pterodroma phaeopygia sandwichensis*	U.S.A. (HI)	E
Pheasant, bar-tailed	*Syrmaticus humaie*	Burma, China	E
Pheasant, Blyth's tragopan	*Tragopan blythii*	Burma, China, India	E
Pheasant, brown-eared	*Crossoptilon mantchuricum*	China	E
Pheasant, Cabot's tragopan	*Tragopan caboti*	do	E
Pheasant, Chinese monal	*Lophophorus lhuysii*	do	E
Pheasant, Edward's	*Lophura edwardsi*	Vietnam	E
Pheasant, Elliot's	*Syrmaticus ellioti*	China	E
Pheasant, imperial	*Lophura imperialis*	Vietnam	E
Pheasant, Mikado	*Syrmaticus mikado*	Taiwan	E
Pheasant, Palawan peacock	*Polyplectron emphanum*	Philippines	E
Pheasant, Sclater's monal	*Lophophorus sclateri*	Burma, China, India	E
Pheasant, Swinhoe's	*Lophura swinhoii*	Taiwan	E
Pheasant, western tragopan	*Tragopan melanocephalus*	India, Pakistan	E
Pheasant, white-eared	*Crossoptilon crossoptilon*	China (Tibet), India	E
Pigeon, Azores wood	*Columba palumbus azorica*	East Atlantic Ocean: Azores.	E
Pigeon, Chatham Island	*Hemiphaga novaeseelandiae chathamensis*	New Zealand	E
Pigeon, Mindoro zone-tailed	*Ducula mindorensis*	Philippines	E
Pigeon, Puerto Rican plain	*Columba inornata wetmorei*	U.S.A. (PR)	E
Piping-guan, black-fronted	*Pipile jacutinga*	Argentina	E
Pitta, Koch's	*Pitta kochi*	Philippines	E
Plover, New Zealand shore	*Thinornis novaeseelandiae*	New Zealand	E
Plover, piping	*Charadrius melodus*	U.S.A. (Great Lakes, northern Great Plains, Atlantic and Gulf Coasts, PR, VI), Canada, Mexico, Bahamas, West Indies.	E

Common name	Scientific name	Location	Status
Po'ouli (honeycreeper)	*Melamprosops phaeosoma*	U.S.A. (HI)	E
Prairie-chicken, Attwater's greater	*Tympanuchus cupido attwateri*	U.S.A. (TX)	E
Quail, Merriam's Montezuma	*Cyrtonyx montezumae merriami*	Mexico (Vera Cruz)	E
Quetzel, resplendent	*Pharomachrus mocinno*	Mexico to Panama	E
Rail, Aukland Island	*Rallus pectoralis muelleri*	New Zealand	E
Rail, California clapper	*Rallus longirostris obsoletus*	U.S.A. (CA)	E
Rail, Guam	*Rallus owstoni*	Western Pacific Ocean: U.S.A. (Guam)	E
Rail, light-footed clapper	*Rllus longirostris levipes*	U.S.A. (CA), Mexico (Baja California)	E
Rail, Lord Howe wood	*Tricholimnas sylvestris*	Australia (Lord Howe Island)	E
Rail, Yuma clapper	*Rallus longirostris yumanensis*	Mexico, U.S.A. (AZ, CA)	E
Rhea, Darwin's	*Pterocnemia pennata*	Argentina, Bolivia, Peru, Uruguay	E
Robin, Chatham Island	*Petroica traversi*	New Zealand	E
Robin, scarlet-breasted (flycatcher)	*Petroica multicolor multicolor*	Australia (Norfolk Island)	E
Rockfowl, grey-necked	*Picathartes oreas*	Cameroon, Gabon	E
Rockfowl, white-necked	*Picathartes gymnocephalus*	Africa: Togo to Sierra Leone	E
Roller, long-tailed ground	*Uratelornis chimaera*	Malagasy Republic (= Madagascar)	E
Scrub-bird, noisy	*Atrichornis clamosus*	Australia	E
Shama, Cebu black (thrush)	*Copsychus niger cebuensis*	Philippines	T
Shearwater, Newell's Townsend's (formerly Manx) (='A'o)	*Puffinus auricularis* (formerly *puffinus*) *newelli*.	U.S.A. (HI)	E
Shrike, San Clemente loggerhead	*Lanius ludovicianus mearnsi*	U.S.A. (CA)	E
Siskin, red	*Carduelis* (= *Spinus*) *cucullata*	South America	E
Sparrow, Cape Sable seaside	*Ammodramus* (= *Ammospiza*) *maritimus mirabilis*.	U.S.A. (FL)	E
Sparrow, dusky seaside	*Ammodramus* (= *Ammospiza*) *maritimus nigrescens*.	do	E
Sparrow, San Clemente sage	*Amphispiza belli clementeae*	U.S.A. (CA)	T
Starling, Ponape mountain	*Aplonis pelzelni*	West Pacific Ocean: U.S.A. (Caroline Islands).	E
Starling, Rothschild's (myna)	*Leucopsar rothschildi*	Indonesia (Bali)	E
Stilt, Hawaiian (= Ae'o)	*Himantopus himantopus knudseni*	U.S.A. (HI)	E
Stork, oriental white	*Ciconia ciconia boyciana*	China, Japan, Korea, U.S.S.R.	E
Stork, wood	*Mycteria americana*	U.S.A., (CA, AZ, TX, to Carolinas), Mexico, Central and South America.	E

Species		Historic range	Status*
Common name	Scientific name		
BIRDS			
Swiftlet, Vanikoro	*Aerodramus (=Collocalia) vanikorensis bartschi*	Western Pacific Ocean: U.S.A. (Guam, Rota, Tinian, Saipan, Agiguan).	E
Teal, Campbell Island flightless	*Anas aucklandica nesiotis*	New Zealand (Campbell Island)	E
Tern, California least	*Sterna antillarum (=albifrons) browni*	Mexico, U.S.A. (CA)	E
Tern, least	*Sterna antillarum*	U.S.A. (Atlantic and Gulf coasts, Miss. R. Basin, CA), Gr. and Lesser Antilles, Bahamas, Mexico; winters C. America, northern S. America.	E
Thrasher, white-breasted	*Ramphocinclus brachyurus*	West Indies: St. Lucia, Martinique	E
Thrush, large Kauai	*Myadestes (= Phaeornis) myadestinus*	W.S.A. (HI)	E
Thrush, Molokai (=oloma'o)	*Myadestes (= Phaeornis) lanaiensis (= obscurus) rutha.*	do	E
Thrush, New Zealand (wattlebird)	*Turnagra capensis*	New Zealand	E
Thrush, small Kauai (= puaiohi)	*Myadestes (= Phaeornis) palmeri*	U.S.A. (HI)	E
Tinamou, solitary	*Tinamus solitarius*	Brazi, Paraguay, Argentina	E
Trembler, Martinique (thrasher)	*Cinclocerthia ruficauda gutturalis*	West Indies: Martinique	E
Wanderer, plain (collared-hemipode)	*Pedionomus torquatus*	Australia	E
Warbler (wood), Bachman's	*Vermivora bachmanii*	U.S.A. (southeastern), Cuba	E
Warbler (wood), Barbados yellow	*Dendroica petechia petechia*	West Indies: Barbados	E
Warbler (wood), Kirtland's	*Dendroica kirtlandii*	U.S.A. (principally MI), Canada, West Indies: Bahama Islands.	E
Warbler (willow), nightingale reed	*Acrocephalus luscinia*	Western Pacific Ocean	E
Warbler (willow), Rodrigues	*Bebrornis rodericanus*	Mauritius (Rodrigues Islands)	E
Warbler (wood), Semper's	*Leucopeza semperi*	West Indies: St. Lucia	E
Warbler (willow), Seychelles	*Bebrornis sechellensis*	Indian Ocean: Seychelles Island	E
Whipbird, Western	*Psophodes nigrogularis*	Australia	E
White-eye, bridled	*Zosterops conspicillata conspicillata*	Western Pacific Ocean: U.S.A. (Guam)	E
White-eye, Norfolk Island	*Zosterops albogularis*	Indian Ocean: Norfolk Islands	E
White-eye, Ponape greater	*Rukia longirostra (= sanfordi)*	West Pacific Ocean: U.S.A. (Caroline Islands).	E

Common name	Scientific name	Range	Status
White-eye, Seychelles	*Zosterops modesta*	Indian Ocean: Seychelles	E
Woodpecker, Imperial	*Campephilus imperialis*	Mexico	E
Woodpecker, ivory-billed	*Campephilus principalis*	U.S.A. (southcentral and southeastern), Cuba.	E
Woodpecker, red-cockaded	*Picoides* (= *Dendrocopos*) *borealis*	U.S.A. (southcentral and southeastern)	E
Woodpecker, Tristam's	*Dryocopus javensis richardsi*	Korea	E
Wren, Guadeloupe house	*Troglodytes aedon guadeloupensis*	West Indies: Guadeloupe	E
Wren, St. Lucia house	*Troglodytes aedon mesoleucus*	West Indies: St. Lucia	E

Reptiles

Common name	Scientific name	Range	Status
Alligator, American	*Alligator mississippiensis*	Southeastern U.S.A.	E
Alligator, Chinese	*Alligator sinensis*	China	E
Anole, Culebra Island giant	*Anolis roosevelti*	U.S.A. (PR: Culebra Island)	E
Boa, Jamaican	*Epicrates subflavus*	Jamaica	E
Boa, Mona	*Epicrates monensis monensis*	U.S.A. (PR)	T
Boa, Puerto Rico	*Epicrates inornatus*	.... do	E
Boa, Round Island [no common name]	*Casarea dussumieri*	Indian Ocean: Mauritius	E
Boa, Round Island [no common name]	*Bolyeria multocarinata*	.... do	E
Boa, Virgin Islands tree	*Epicrates monensis granti*	U.S. and British Virgin Islands	E
Caiman, Apaporis River	*Caiman crocodilus apaporiensis*	Colombia	E
Caiman, black	*Melanosuchus niger*	Amazon basin	E
Caiman, broad-snouted	*Caiman latirostris*	Brazil, Argentina, Paraguay, Uruguay	E
Caiman, Yacare	*Caiman crocodilus yacare*	Bolivia, Argentina, Peru, Brazil	E
Chuckwalla, San Esteban Island	*Sauromalus varius*	Mexico	E
Crocodile, African dwarf	*Osteolaemus tetraspis tetraspis*	West Africa	E
Crocodile, African slender-snouted	*Crocodylus cataphractus*	Western and central Africa	E
Crocodile, American	*Crocodylus acutus*	U.S.A. (FL), Mexico, South America, Central America, Caribbean.	E
Crocodile, Ceylon mugger	*Crocodylus palustris kimbula*	Sri Lanka	E
Crocodile, Congo dwarf	*Osteolaemus tetraspis osborni*	Congo River drainage	E
Crocodile, Cuban	*Crocodylus rhombifer*	Cuba	E
Crocodile, Morelet's	*Crocodylus moreletii*	Mexico, Belize, Guatemala	E
Crocodile, mugger	*Crocodylus palustris palustris*	India, Pakistan, Iran, Bangladesh	E

Species		Historic range	Status*
Common name	Scientific name		
REPTILES			
Crocodile, Nile	*Crocodylus niloticus*	Africa	E
Crocodile, Orinoco	*Crocodylus intermedius*	South America: Orinoco River Basin	E
Crocodile, Philippine	*Crocodylus novaeguineae mindorensis*	Philippine Islands	E
Crocodile, saltwater (=estuarine)	*Crocodylus porosus*	Southeast Asia, Australia, Papua-New Guinea, Pacific Islands.	E
Crocodile, Siamese	*Crocodylus siamensis*	Southeast Asia, Malay Peninsula	E
Gavial (=gharial)	*Gavialis gangeticus*	Pakistan, Burma, Bangladesh, India, Nepal.	E
Gecko, day	*Phelsuma edwardnewtoni*	Indian Ocean: Mauritius	E
Gecko, Monito	*Sphaerodactylus micropithecus*	U.S.A. (PR)	E
Gecko, Round Island day	*Phelsuma guentheri*	Indian Ocean: Mauritius	E
Gecko, Serpent Island	*Cyrtodactylus serpensinula*	do	T
Iguana, Acklins ground	*Cyclura rileyi nuchalis*	West Indies: Bahamas	T
Iguana, Allen's Cay	*Cyclura cychlura inornata*	do	T
Iguana, Andros Island ground	*Cyclura cychlura cychlura*	do	T
Iguana, Anegada ground	*Cyclura pinguis*	West Indies: British Virgin Islands (Anegada Islands).	E
Iguana, Barrington land	*Conolophus pallidus*	Ecuador (Galapagos Islands)	E
Iguana, Cayman Brac ground	*Cyclura nubila caymanensis*	West Indies: Cayman Islands	T
Iguana, Cuba ground	*Cyclura nubila nubila*	Cuba	T
Iguana, Exuma Island	*Cyclura cychlura figginsi*	West Indies: Bahamas	T
Iguana, Fiji banded	*Brachylophus fasciatus*	Pacific: Fiji, Tonga	E
Iguana, Fiji crested	*Brachylophus vitiensis*	Pacific: Fiji	E
Iguana, Grand Cayman ground	*Cyclura nubila lewisi*	West Indies: Cayman Islands	E
Iguana, Jamaican	*Cyclura collei*	West Indies: Jamaica.	E
Iguana, Mayaguana	*Cyclura carinata bartschi*	West Indies: Bahamas	T
Iguana, Mona ground	*Cyclura stejnegeri*	U.S.A. (PR: Mona Island)	T
Iguana, Turks and Caicos	*Cyclura carinata carinata*	West Indies: Turks and Caicos Islands.	T
Iguana, Watling Island ground	*Cyclura rileyi rileyi*	West Indies: Bahamas	E
Iguana, White Cay ground	*Cyclura rileyi cristata*	do	T

Common name	Scientific name	Distribution	Status
Lizard, blunt-nosed leopard	Gambelia (= Crotaphytus) silus	U.S.A. (CA)	E
Lizard, Coachella Valley fringe-toed	Uma inornata	....do....	T
Lizard, Hierro giant	Gallotia simonyi simonyi	Spain (Canary Islands)	E
Lizard, Ibiza wall	Podarcis pityusensis	Spain (Balearic Islands)	T
Lizard, Island night	Xantusia (= Klauberina) riversiana	U.S.A. (CA)	T
Lizard, St. Croix ground	Ameiva polops	U.S.A. (VI)	E
Monitor, Bengal	Varanus bengalensis	Iran, Iraq, India, Sri Lanka, Malaysia, Afghanistan, Burma, Vietnam, Thailand.	E
Monitor, desert	Varanus griseus	North Africa to Neareast, Caspian Sea through U.S.S.R. to Pakistan, Northwest India.	E
Monitor, Komodo Island	Varanus komodoensis	Indonesia (Komodo, Rintja, Padar, and western Flores Island).	E
Monitor, yellow	Varanus flavescens	West Pakistan through India to Bangladesh.	E
Python, Indian	Python molurus molurus	Sri Lanka and India	E
Rattlesnake, Aruba Island	Crotalus unicolor	Aruba Island (Netherland Antilles)	T
Rattlesnake, New Mexico ridge-nosed	Crotalus willardi obscurus	U.S.A. (NM), Mexico	T
Skink, Round Island	Leiolopisma telfairi	Indian Ocean: Mauritius	T
Snake, Atlantic salt marsh	Nerodia fasciata taeniata	U.S.A. (FL)	T
Snake, eastern indigo	Drymarchon corais couperi	U.S.A. (AL, FL, GA, MS, SC)	T
Snake, San Francisco garter	Thamnophis sirtalis tetrataenia	U.S.A. (CA)	E
Tartaruga	Podocnemis expansa	South America: Orinoco and Amazon River basins.	E
Terrapin, river (= Tuntong)	Batagur baska	Malaysia, Bangladesh, Burma, India, Indonesia.	E
Tomistoma	Tomistoma schlegelii	Malaysia, Indonesia	E
Tortoise, angulated	Geochelone yniphora	Malagasy Republic (= Madagascar)	E
Tortoise, Bolson	Gopherus flavomarginatus	Mexico	E
Tortoise, desert	Scaptochelys (= Gopherus) agassizii	U.S.A. (UT, AZ, CA, NV); Mexico	T
Tortoise, Galapagos	Geochelone elephantopus	Ecuador (Galapagos Islands)	E
Tortoise, radiated	Geochelone (= Testudo) radiata	Malagasy Republic (= Madagascar)	E
Tracaja	Podocnemis unifilis	South America: Orinoco and Amazon River basins.	E

Species		Historic range	Status*
Common name	Scientific name		

REPTILES

Common name	Scientific name	Historic range	Status*
Tuatara	*Sphenodon punctatus*	New Zealand	E
Turtle, aquatic box	*Terrapene coahuila*	Mexico	E
Turtle, black softshell	*Trionyx nigricans*	Bangladesh	E
Turtle, Burmese peacock	*Morenia ocellata*	Burma	E
Turtle, Central American river	*Dermatemys mawii*	Mexico, Belize, Guatemala	E
Turtle, Cuatro Cienegas softshell	*Trionyx ater*	Mexico	E
Turtle, geometric	*Psammobates geometricus (= Geochelone geometrica).*	South Africa	E
Turtle, green sea	*Chelonia mydas*	Circumglobal in tropical and temperate seas and oceans.	T
Turtle, hawksbill sea (= carey)	*Eretmochelys imbricata.*	Tropical seas	E
Turtle, Indian sawback	*Kachuga tecta tecta*	India	E
Turtle, Indian softshell	*Trionyx gangeticus*	Pakistan, India	E
Turtle, Kemp's (= Atlantic) Ridley sea	*Lepidochelys kempii*	Tropical and temperate seas in Atlantic Basin.	E
Turtle, leatherback sea	*Dermochelys coriacea*	Tropical, temperate, and subpolar seas	E
Turtle, loggerhead sea	*Caretta caretta*	Circumglobal in tropical and temperate seas and oceans.	T
Turtle, Olive (Pacific) Ridley sea	*Lepidochelys olivacea*	Tropical and temperate seas in Pacific Basin.	T
Turtle, peacock softshell	*Trionyx hurum*	India, Bangladesh	E
Turtle, Plymouth red-bellied	*Pseudemys (= Chrysemys) rubriventris bangsi.*	U.S.A. (MA)	E
Turtle, short-necked or western swamp	*Pseudemydura umbrina*	Australia	E
Turtle, spotted pond	*Geoclemys (= Damonia) hamiltonii*	North India, Pakistan	E
Turtle, three-keeled Asian	*Melanochelys (= Geoemyda, Nicoria) tricarinata.*	Central India to Bangladesh and Burma	E
Viper, Lar Valley	*Vipera latifii*	Iran	E

AMPHIBIANS

Common name	Scientific name	Location	Status
Coqui, golden	*Eleutherodactylus jasperi*	U.S.A. (PR)	T
Frog, Israel painted	*Discoglossus nigriventer*	Israel	E
Frog, Panamanian golden	*Atelopus varius zeteki*	Panama	E
Frog, Stephen Island	*Leiopelma hamiltoni*	New Zealand	E
Salamander, Chinese giant	*Andrias davidianus davidianus*	Western China	E
Salamander, desert slender	*Batrachoseps aridus*	U.S.A.(CA)	E
Salamander, Japanese giant	*Andrias davidianus japonicus*	Japan	E
Salamander, Red Hills	*Phaeognathus hubrichti*	U.S.A. (AL)	T
Salamander, San Marcos	*Eurycea nana*	U.S.A. (TX)	T
Salamander, Santa Cruz long-toed	*Ambystoma macrodactylum croceum*	U.S.A. (CA)	E
Salamander, Texas blind	*Typhlomolge rathbuni*	U.S.A. (TX)	E
Toad, Africana viviparous	*Nectophrynoides* spp.	Tanzania, Guinea, Ivory Coast, Cameroon, Liberia, Ethiopia.	E
Toad, Cameroon	*Bufo superciliaris*	Equatorial Africa	E
Toad, Houston	*Bufo houstonensis*	U.S.A. (TX)	E
Toad, Monte Verde	*Bufo periglenes*	Costa Rica	E
Toad, Wyoming	*Bufo hemiophrys baxteri*	U.S.A. (WY)	E

FISHES

Common name	Scientific name	Location	Status
Ala Balik (trout)	*Salmo platycephalus*	Turkey	E
Ayurnodoki (loach)	*Hymenophysa (= Botia) curta*	Japan	E
Blindcat, Mexican (catfish)	*Prietella phreatophila*	Mexico	E
Bonytoungue, Asian	*Scleropages formosus*	Thailand, Indonesia, Malaysia	E
Catfish [no common name]	*Pangasius sanitwongsei*	Thailand	E
Catfish, giant	*Pangasianodon gigas*	do	T
Catfish, Yaqui	*Ictalurus pricei*	U.S.A. (AZ), Mexico.	T
Cavefish, Alabama	*Speoplatyrhinus poulsoni*	U.S.A. (AL)	T
Cavefish, Ozark	*Amblyopsis rosae*	U.S.A. (AR, MO, OK)	T
Chub, bonytail	*Gila elegans*	U.S.A. (AZ, CA, CO, NV, UT, WY)	E
Chub, Borax Lake	*Gila boraxobius*	U.S.A. (OR)	E
Chub, Chihuahua	*Gila nigrescens*	U.S.A. (NM), Mexico (Chihuahua)	T

Species		Historic range	Status*
Common name	Scientific name		
FISHES			
Chub, humpback	*Gila cypha*	U.S.A. (AX, CO, UT, WY)	E
Chub, Hutton tui	*Gila bicolor ssp*	U.S.A. (OR)	T
Chub, Mohave tui	*Gila bicolor mohavensis*	U.S.A. (CA)	E
Chub, Owens tui	*Gila bicolor snyderi*	do	E
Chub, Pahranagat roundtail	*Gila robusta jordani*	U.S.A. (NV)	E
Chub, slender	*Hybopsis cahni*	U.S.A. (TN, VA)	T
Chub, spotfin	*Hybopsis monacha*	U.S.A. (AL, GA, NC, TN, VA)	T
Chub, Yaqui	*Gila purpurea*	U.S.A. (AZ), Mexico	E
Cicek (minnow)	*Acanthorutilus handlirschi*	Turkey	E
Cui-ui	*Chasmistes cujus*	U.S.A. (NV)	E
Dace, Ash Meadows speckled	*Rhinichthys osculus nevadensis*	do	E
Dace, desert	*Eremichthys acros*	do	T
Dace, Foskett speckled	*Rhinichthys osculus ssp*	U.S.A. (OR)	T
Dace, Kendall Warm Springs	*Rhinichthys osculus thermalis*	U.S.A. (WY)	E
Dace, Moapa	*Moapa coriacea*	U.S.A. (NV)	E
Darter, amber	*Percina antesella*	U.S.A. (GA, TN)	E
Darter, bayou	*Etheostoma rubrum*	U.S.A. (MS)	T
Darter, fountain	*Etheostoma fonticola*	U.S.A. (TX)	E
Darter, leopard	*Percina pantherina*	U.S.A. (AR, OK)	T
Darter, Maryland	*Etheostoma sellare*	U.S.A. (MD)	E
Darter, Niangua	*Etheostoma nianguae*	U.S.A. (MO)	T
Darter, Okaloosa	*Etheostoma okaloosae*	U.S.A. (FL)	E
Darter, slackwater	*Etheostoma boschungi*	U.S.A. (AL, TN)	T
Darter, snail	*Percina tanasi*	U.S.A. (AL, GA, TN)	T
Darter, watercress	*Etheostoma nuchale*	U.S.A. (AL)	E
Gambusia, Big Bend	*Gambusia gaigei*	U.S.A. (TX)	E
Gambusia, Clear Creek	*Gambusia heterochir*	do	E
Gambusia, Amistad	*Gambusia amistadensis*	do	E
Gambusia, Pecos	*Gambusia nobilis*	U.S.A. (NM,TX)	E

Killifish, Pahrump	*Empetrichthys latos*	U.S.A. (NV)	E
Logperch, Conasauga	*Percina jenkinsi*	U.S.A. (GA, TN)	E
Madtom, Scioto	*Noturus trautmani*	U.S.A. (OH)	E
Madtom, Smoky	*Noturus baileyi*	U.S.A. (TN)	T
Madtom, yellowfin	*Noturus flavipinnis*	U.S.A. (GA, TN, VA)	E
Nekogigi (catfish)	*Coreobagrus ichikawai*	Japan	E
Pupfish, Ash Meadows Amargosa	*Cyprinodon nevadensis mionectes*	U.S.A. (NV)	E
Pupfish, Comanche Springs	*Cyprinodon elegans*	U.S.A. (TX)	E
Pupfish, Devils Hole	*Cyprinodon diabolis*	U.S.A. (NV)	E
Pupfish, Leon Springs	*Cyprinodon bovinus*	U.S.A. (TX)	E
Pupfish, Owens	*Cyprinodon radiosus*	U.S.A. (CA)	E
Pupfish, Warm Springs	*Cyprinodon nevadensis pectoralis*	U.S.A. (NV)	E
Shiner, beautiful	*Notropis formosus*	U.S.A. (AZ, NM), Mexico	T
Spinedace, Big Spring	*Lepidomeda mollispinis pratensis*	U.S.A. (NV)	T
Spinedace, White River	*Lepidomeda albivallis*	do.	E
Springfish, Hiko White River	*Crenichthys baileyi grandis*	do.	E
Springfish, White River	*Crenichthys baileyi baileyi*	do.	E
Squawfish, Colorado	*Ptychocheilus lucius*	U.S.A. (AZ, CA, CO, NM, NV, UT, WY), Mexico.	E
Stickleback, unarmored threespine	*Gasterosteus aculeatus williamsoni*	U.S.A. (CA)	E
Sturgeon, shortnose	*Acipenser brevirostrum*	U.S.A. and Canada (Atlantic Coast)	E
Sucker, Modoc	*Catostomus microps*	U.S.A. (CA)	E
Sucker, Warner	*Catostomus warnerensis*	U.S.A. (OR)	T
Tango, Miyako (Tokyo bitterling)	*Tanakia tango*	Japan	E
Temolek, Ikan (minnow)	*Probarbus jullieni*	Thailand, Cambodia, Vietnam, Malaysia, Laos.	E
Topminnow, Gila	*Poeciliopsis occidentalis*	U.S.A. (AZ, NM), Mexico	E
Totoaba (seatrout or weakfish)	*Cynoscion macdonaldi*	Mexico (Gulf of California)	E
Trout, Apache	*Salmo apache*	U.S.A. (AZ)	T
Trout, Gila	*Salmo gilae*	U.S.A. (AX, NM)	E
Trout, greenback cutthroat	*Salmo clarki stomias*	U.S.A. (CO)	T
Trout, Lahontan cutthroat	*Salmo clarki henshawi*	U.S.A. (CA, NV)	T
Trout, Little Kern golden	*Salmo aguabonita whitei*	U.S.A. (CA)	T
Trout, Paiute cutthroat	*Salmo clarki seleniris*	do.	T
Woundfin	*Plagopterus argentissimus*	U.S.A. (AZ, NV, UT)	E

APPENDIX II
ENDANGERED AND THREATENED PLANTS

Species		Historic range	Status
Scientific name	Common name		
Agavaceae—Agave family:			
Agave arizonica	Arizona agave	U.S.A. (AZ)	E
Alismataceae—Water-plantain family:			
Sagittaria fasciculata	Bunched arrowhead	U.S.A. (NC, SC)	E
Apiaceae—Parsley family:			
Eryngium constancei	Loch Lomond coyote-thistle	U.S.A. (CA)	E
Asteraceae—Aster family:			
Bidens cuneata	Cuneate bidens	U.S.A. (HI)	E
Dyssodia tephroleuca	Ashy dogweed	U.S.A. (TX)	E
Echinacea tennesseensis	Tennessee purple coneflower	U.S.A. (TN)	E
Enceliopsis nudicaulis var. corrugata	Ash Meadows sunray	U.S.A. (NV)	T
Erigeron maguirei var. maguirei	Maguire daisy	U.S.A. (UT)	E
Erigeron rhizomatus	Rhizome fleabane	U.S.A. (NM)	T
Grindelia fraxinopratensis	Ash Meadows gumplant	U.S.A. (CA, NV)	T
Lipochaeta venosa	None	U.S.A. (HI)	E
Pityopsis ruthii (= Heterotheca ruthii, = Chrysopsis ruthii)	Ruth's golden aster	U.S.A. (TN)	E
Senecio franciscanus	San Francisco Peaks groundsel	U.S.A. (AZ)	T
Solidago shortii	Short's goldenrod	U.S.A. (KY)	E
Solidago spithamaea	Blue Ridge goldenrod	U.S.A. (NC, TN)	T
Stephanomeria malheurensis	Malheur wire-lettuce	U.S.A. (OR)	E
Townsendia aprica	Last Chance townsendia	U.S.A. (UT)	T
Berberidaceae—Barberry family:			
Mahonia sonnei (= Berberis s.)	Truckee barberry	U.S.A. (CA)	E
Betulaceae—Birch family:			
Betula uber	Virginia round-leaf birch	U.S.A. (VA)	E

	Common name	Location	Status
Boraginaceae—Borage family:			
Amsinckia grandiflora	Large-flowered fiddleneck	U.S.A. (CA)	E
Brassicaceae—Mustard family:			
Arabis mcdonaldiana	McDonald's rock-cress	U.S.A. (CA)	E
Erysimum capitatum var. *angustatum*	Contra Costa wallflower	do	E
Thelypodium stenopetalum	Slender-petaled mustard	do	E
Buxaceae—Boxwood family:			
Buxus vahlii	Vahl's boxwood	U.S.A. (PR)	E
Cactaceae—Cactus family:			
Ancistrocactus tobuschii (= *Echinocactus t.*, *Mammillaria t.*).	Tobusch fishhook cactus	U.S.A. (TX)	E
Cereus eriophorus var. *fragrans*	Fragrant prickly-apple	U.S.A. (FL)	E
Cereus robinii	Key tree-cactus	U.S.A. (FL), Cuba	E
Coryphantha minima (= *C. nellieae*, *Escobaria n.*, *Mammillaria n.*).	Nellie cory cactus	U.S.A. (TX)	E
Coryphantha ramillosa	Bunched cory cactus	U.S.A. (TX), Mexico (Coahuila).	T
Coryphantha sneedii var. *leei* (= *Escobaria l.*, *Mammillaria l.*).	Lee pincushion cactus	U.S.A. (NM)	T
Coryphantha sneedii var. *sneedii* (= *Escobaria s.*, *Mammillaria s.*).	Sneed pincushion cactus	U.S.A. (TX, NM)	E
Echinocactus horizonthalonius var. *nicholii*	Nichol's Turk's head cactus	U.S.A. (AZ)	E
Echinocereus engelmannii var. *purpureus*	Purple-spined hedgehog cactus	U.S.A. (UT)	E
Echinocereus fendleri var. *kuenzleri* (= *E. kunzleri*, *E. hempelii* of authors, not Fobe).	Kuenzler hedgehog cactus	U.S.A. (NM)	E
Echinocereus lloydii (= *E. roetteri* var. *l.*)	Lloyd's hedgehog cactus	U.S.A. (TX)	E
Echinocereus reichenbachii var. *albertii* (= *E. melanocentrus*).	Black lace cactus	do	E
Echinocereus triglochidiatus var. *arizonicus* (= *E. arizonicus*).	Arizona hedgehog cactus	U.S.A. (AZ)	E
Echinocereus triglochidiatus var. *inermis* (= *E. coccineus* var. *i.*, *E. phoeniceus* var. *i.*).	Spineless hedgehog cactus	U.S.A. (CO, UT)	E

—119—

Species		Historic range	Status
Scientific name	Common name		
Echinocereus viridiflorus var. (= *E. davisii*)	Davis' green pitaya	U.S.A. (TX)	E
Neolloydia mariposensis (= *Echinocactus m., Echinomastus m.*).	Lloyd's Mariposa cactus	U.S.A. (TX), Mexico (Coahuila).	T
Pediocactus bradyi (= *Toumeya b.*)	Brady pincushion cactus	U.S.A. (AZ)	E
Pediocactus knowltonii (= *P. bradyi* var. *k. Toumeya k.*).	Knowlton cactus	U.S.A. (NM, CO)	E
Pediocactus peeblesianus var. *peeblesianus* (= *Echinocactus p., Navajoa p., Toumeya p., Utahia p.*).	Peebles Navajo cactus	U.S.A. (AZ)	E
Pediocactus sileri (= *Echinocactus s., Utahia s.*).	Siler pincushion cactus	U.S.A. (AZ, UT)	E
Sclerocactus glaucus (= *Echinocactus g., E. subglaucus, E. whipplei* var. *g., Pediocactus g., S. franklinii, S. whipplei* var. *g.*).	Uinta Basin hookless cactus	U.S.A. (CO, UT)	T
Sclerocactus mesae-verdae (= *Coloradoa m., Echinocactus m., Pediocactus m.*).	Mesa Verde cactus	U.S.A. (CO, NM)	T
Sclerocactus wrightiae (= *Pediocactus w.*).	Wright fishhook cactus	U.S.A. (UT)	E
Caryophyllaceae—Pink family: *Schiedea adamantis*	Diamond Head schiedea	U.S.A. (HI)	E
Chenopodiaceae—Goosefoot family: *Nitrophila mohavensis*	Amargosa nitrewort	U.S.A. (CA)	E
Cistaceae—Rockrose family: *Hudsonia montana*	Mountain golden heather	U.S.A. (NC)	T
Crassulaceae—Stonecrop family: *Dudleya traskiae*	Santa Barbara Island liveforever	U.S.A. (CA)	E
Cupressaceae—Cyprus family: *Fitzroya cupressoides*	Chilen false larch (= alerce)	Chile, Argentina	T

	Common name	Location	Status
Cyperaceae—Sedge family:			
Carex specuicola	None	U.S.A. (AZ)	T
Ericaceae—Heath family:			
Arctostaphylos pungens var. *ravenii* (= *A. hookeri* ssp. *ravenii*)	Presidio (= Raven's) manzanita	U.S.A. (CA)	E
Rhododendron chapmanii	Chapman rhododendron	U.S.A. (FL)	E
Euphorbiaceae—Spurge family:			
Euphorbia (= *Chamaesyce*) *deltoidea* ssp. *deltoidea*.	Spurge	U.S.A. (FL)	E
Euphorbia (= *Chamaesyce*) *garberi*	None	........do	T
Euphorbia skottsbergii var. *kalaeloana*	Ewa Plains 'akoko	U.S.A. (HI)	E
Jatropha costaricensis	Costa Rica jatropha	Costa Rica	E
Fabaceae—Pea family:			
Amorpha crenulata	Crenulate lead-plant	U.S.A. (FL)	E
Astragalus humillimus	Mancos milk-vetch	U.S.A. (CO, NM)	E
Astragalus perianus	Rydberg milk-vetch	U.S.A. (UT)	T
Astragalus phoenix	Ash Meadows milk-vetch	U.S.A. (NV)	T
Baptisia arachnifera	Hairy rattleweed	U.S.A. (GA)	E
Galactia smallii	Small's milkpea	U.S.A. (FL)	E
Hoffmannseggia tenella	Slender rush-pea	U.S.A. (TX)	E
Lotus dendroideus ssp. *traskiae* (= *L. scoparius* ssp. *t.*).	San Clemente Island broom	U.S.A. (CA)	E
Vicia menziesii	Hawaiian vetch	U.S.A. (HI)	E
Frankeniaceae—Frankenia family:			
Frankenia johnstonii	Johnston's frankenia	U.S.A. (TX), Mexico (Nuevo Leon).	E
Gentianaceae—Gentian family:			
Centaurium namophilum	Spring-loving centaury	U.S.A. (CA, NV)	T
Hydrophyllaceae—Waterleaf family:			
Phacelia agrillacea	Clay phacelia	U.S.A. (UT)	E
Phacelia formosula	North Park phacelia	U.S.A. (CO)	E

Species		Historic range	Status
Scientific name	Common name		
Lamiaceae—Mint family:			
Acanthomintha obovata ssp. *duttonii*	San Mateo thornmint	U.S.A. (CA)	E
Dicerandra cornutissima	Longspurred mint	U.S.A. (FL)	E
Dicerandra frutescens	Scrub mint	do	E
Dicerandra immaculata	Lakela's mint	do	E
Haplostachys haplostachya var. *angustifolia*	None	U.S.A. (HI)	E
Hedeoma apiculatum	McKittrick pennyroyal	U.S.A. (TX, NM)	T
Hedeoma todsenii	Todsen's pennyroyal	U.S.A. (NM)	E
Pogogyne abramsii	San Diego mesa mint	U.S.A. (CA)	E
Stenogyne angustifolia var. *angustifolia*	None	U.S.A. (HI)	E
Liliaceae—Lily family:			
Harperocallis flava	Harper's beauty	U.S.A. (FL)	E
Trillium persistens	Persistent rillium	U.S.A. (GA, SC)	E
Loasaceae—Loasa family:			
Mentzelia leucophylla	Ash Meadows blazing star	U.S.A. (NV)	T
Malvaceae—Mallow family:			
Callirhoe scabriuscala	Texas poppy-mallow	U.S.A. (TX)	E
Kokia cookei	Cooke's kokio	U.S.A. (HI)	E
Kokia drynarioides	Koki'o (= hau-hele'ula or Hawaii tree cotton)	do	E
Malacothamnus clementinus	San Clemente Island bush-mallow	U.S.A. (CA)	E
Sidalcea pedata	Pedate checker-mallow	do	E
Nyctaginaceae—Four-o'clock family:			
Mirabilis macfarlanei	MacFarlane's four-o'clock	U.S.A. (ID, OR)	E
Onagraceae—Evening-primrose family:			
Camissonia benitensis	San Benito evening-primrose	U.S.A. (CA)	T
Oenothera avita ssp. *eurekensis*	Eureka Valley evening-primrose	do	E
Oenothera deltoides ssp. *howellii*	Antioch Dunes evening-primrose	do	E

Orchidaceae—Orchid family:			
Isotria medeoloides	Small whorled pogonia	U.S.A. (CT, IL, MA, MD, ME, MI, MO, NC, NH, NJ, NY, PA, RI, SC, VA, VT), Canada (Ont.).	E
Spiranthes parksii	Navasota ladies'-tresses	U.S.A. (TX)	E
Papaveraceae—Poppy family:			
Arctomecon humilis	Dwarf bear-poppy	U.S.A. (UT)	E
Pinaceae—Pine family:			
Abies guatemalensis	Guatemalan fir (= pinabete)	Mexico, Guatemala, Honduras, El Salvador	T
Poaceae—Grass family:			
Tuctoria mucronata (= *Orcuttia m.*)	Solano grass	U.S.A. (CA)	E
Panicum carteri	Carter's panicgrass	U.S.A. (HI)	E
Swallenia alexandrae	Eureka Dune grass	U.S.A. (CA)	E
Zizania texana	Texas wild-rice	U.S.A. (TX)	E
Polygalaceae—Milkwort family:			
Polygala smallii	Tiny polygala	U.S.A. (FL)	E
Polygonaceae—Buckwheat family:			
Eriogonum gypsophilum	Gypsum wild-buckwheat	U.S.A. (NM)	T
Eriogonum pelinophilum	Clay-loving wild-buckwheat	U.S.A. (CO)	E
Primulaceae—Primrose family:			
Primula maguirei	Maguire primrose	U.S.A. (UT)	T
Ranunculaceae—Buttercup family:			
Aconitum noveboracense	Northern wild monkshood	U.S.A. (IA, NY, OH, WI).	T
Delphinium kinkiense	San Clemente Island larkspur	U.S.A. (CA)	E

Species		Historic range	Status
Scientific name	Common name		
Rhamnaceae—Buckhorn family:			
Gouania hillebrandii	None	U.S.A. (HI)	E
Rosaceae—Rose family:			
Cowania subintegra	Arizona cliffrose	U.S.A. (AZ)	E
Ivesia eremica	Ash Meadows ivesia	U.S.A. (NV)	T
Potentilla robbinsiana	Robbins' cinquefoil	U.S.A. (NH, VT)	E
Rubiaceae—Coffee family:			
Gardenia brighamii	Na'u (Hawaiian gardenia)	U.S.A. (HI)	E
Rutaceae—Citrus family:			
Zanthoxylum thomasianum	Prickly-ash	U.S.A. (PR, VI)	E
Sarraceniaceae—Pitcher plant family:			
Sarracenia oreophila	Green pitcher plant	U.S.A. (AL, GA, TN)	E
Saxifragaceae—Saxifrage family:			
Ribes echinellum	Miccosukee gooseberry	U.S.A. (FL, SC)	T
Scrophulariaceae—Snapdragon family:			
Castilleja grisea	San Clemente Island Indian paintbrush	U.S.A. (CA)	E
Cordylanthus maritimus ssp. *maritimus*	Salt marsh bird's-beak	U.S.A. (CA), Mexico (Baja California)	E
Pediculans furbisshiane	Furbish lousewort	U.S.A. (ME), Canada (New Brunswick)	E
Solanaceae—Nightshade family:			
Goetzea elegans	Beautiful goetzea, matabuey	U.S.A. (PR)	E
Styracaceae—Styrax family:			
Styrax texana	Texas snowbells	U.S.A. (TX)	E
Taxaceae—Yew family:			
Torreya taxifolia	Florida torreya	U.S.A. (FL, GA)	E

INDEX